FINDING YOUR WAY

NAVIGATING LIFE BY UNDERSTANDING
YOUR LEARNING SELF

---

*FEATURING THE LET ME LEARN PROCESS®, AN
ADVANCED LEARNING SYSTEM*

CHRISTINE A. JOHNSTON ED.D.

For information about permission to reproduce selections from this book, write to *Permissions, Let Me Learn, Inc., 31 Driftwood Court, Glassboro, NJ 08028*

For information about special discount for bulk purchases, please contact info@*letmelearn.org*

Johnston, Christine A.
Finding Your Way: Navigating Life by Understanding Your Learning Self
Includes bibliographical references, glossary, and index.
ISBN: 1451549563
ISBN-13: 9781451549560
1. Adult Learner. 2. Learning. 3. Learning strategies. 4. Self-help
Library of Congress Control Number: 2010910068

Let Me Learn, Inc. 31 Driftwood Court, Glassboro, NJ 08028
www.letmelearn.org

This book is dedicated to Colin Calleja, friend and colleague who from LML's inception caught its spirit and message and made the commitment to help others find a Compass Rose of Learning to navigate their work world and personal life more successfully.

This book is also dedicated to my nine grandchildren—Emily, David, Stephanie, Meredith, Noah, Connor, Ella, Quinn, and Eve—in the hope that they will find their True North, navigate the global crosswinds of the 21st century, and use their individual Compass Rose to come safe home.

Contents

List of Figures...vii

Foreword: *Noreen C. Campbell*..*xi*

Acknowledgments...xv

Introduction "But I Didn't Know I Was Lost!"...........xvii

Part I: Finding Your Way: Setting the Course xxiii

1. Examining the Coordinates of Your Life 1

2. Recognizing the Importance of Your Compass
   Rose..13

3. Boxing Your Compass Rose 27

Part II: Finding Your Way: Staying the Course.........57

4. All Hands on Deck 59

5. Adrift in Uncharted Waters......................................79

6. Assuming the Helm for Success 109

Part III: Finding Your Way: Safe Home! 125

7. Navigating the Flat World of the 21st Century........127

The Reprise "Are We There Yet?"..............................141

Appendix A: LCI (Learning Connection Inventory)....147

Appendix B: Recognizing Learning Patterns at Work...157

Glossary 159

References and Suggested Readings.............................169

About the Author 175

Index 177

LIST OF FIGURES

Front Material

    Figure i Compass Rose 1 xvii

Chapter 1

    Figure 1.1 Compass Rose 2 1

Chapter 2

    Figure 2.1 Compass Rose 3 13

    Figure 2.2 Personal Compass Rose 25

Chapter 3

    Figure 3.1 Compass Rose 27

    Figure 3.2 Brain-Mind Connection 30

    Figure 3.3 Range of LCI Scale Scores 37

    Figure 3.4 Use First Sequence 39

    Figure 3.5 Avoid Sequence 39

    Figure 3.6 Use First Precision 40

    Figure 3.7 Avoid Precision 41

    Figure 3.8 Use First Technical Reasoning 42

    Figure 3.9 Avoid Technical Reasoning 42

    Figure 3.10 Use First Confluence 43

    Figure 3.11 Avoid Confluence 44

    Figure 3.12 Sample Responses Dynamic Learner I 45

    Figure 3.13 Sample Responses Dynamic Learner II 46

    Figure 3.14 Sample Responses Strong-willed Learner ... 47

Figure 3.15 Sample Responses Bridge Learner 48

Figure 3.16 Description of My Personal Compass
        Rose (Sample) 55

Figure 3.17 Description of My Personal Compass
        Rose (Blank) 56

Chapter 4

Figure 4.1 Compass Rose 5 59

Figure 4.2 Metacognitive Drill 66

Chapter 5

Figure 5.1 Compass Rose 6 79

Figure 5.2 Decoded Procedures for Plant Operators 87

Figure 5.3 Directional Forces Word Wall 89

Figure 5.4 Decoded Task I 90

Figure 5.5 Decoding Task II 91

Figure 5.6 Decoding Task III 93

Figure 5.7 Sample Personal Directional Forces
        Strategy Card 101

Figure 5.8 Personal Directional Forces Strategy
        Card Blank 105

Figure 5.9 Worksite Strategies S-P 106

Figure 5.10 Worksite Strategies T-C 107

Chapter 6

Figure 6.1 Compass Rose 7 109

Chapter 7

Figure 7.1 Compass Rose 8 127

Figure 7.2 My Personal Chart for Navigating the
Flat World..139

Reprise

Figure R.1 Compass Rose 9...141

Appendix A

Figure A.1 Modified LCI Score Sheet...........................156

Appendix B

Figure B.1 Recognizing Learning Patterns at Work....157

FOREWORD

I think *Finding Your Way: Navigating Life by Understanding Your Learning Self* is the most important work to be published in business literature in the past 20 years. I make this bold statement because I have always approached work with a deep conviction that individual development is the key to organizational success and that, as a supervisor, developing my subordinates was essential to my success. It wasn't until I was introduced to the practical theory of learning outlined in this book that I found the secret to helping others improve their learning success in many different situations. My experience with this learning theory has demonstrated its straightforward applications to the world of work.

Why Is Learning so Important Today?

In Peter Senge's seminal work, *The Fifth Discipline: The Art and Practice of the Learning Organization* (1990), he identified that in situations of rapid change, only those organizations that are flexible, adaptive, and productive will excel—only learning organizations with individuals who are able to learn quickly and adapt will survive. Never before have these words carried the impact they do today. At this junction in our nation's economic history, employers and employees of all ilk are confronted both by the globalization of our economy and the recession caused by the financial crisis of 2008–2009, resulting in millions of talented, hardworking people losing their jobs. Through no fault of their own, they have found themselves adrift in uncharted waters, looking for work in an economy that threatens to shipwreck them on the rocks of change. It can easily be argued that individuals who are aware of how to use their learning selves effectively will have the best chance for keeping their heads above the rising waters of the current chaotic situation that is today's global marketplace.

Why Is This Learning Theory Different?

I first met the author of *Finding Your Way*, Chris Johnston, when I was managing a small chemical plant that was in the process of shutting down one of its two manufacturing operations. Over a 12-month period, the plant was going to lose half of its current employees. While one operation was shutting down, the other operation needed to continue to manufacture and deliver a quality critical product to a demanding customer. Although half of the remaining employees were going to have to change jobs within the plant and were going to require retraining, we could not afford to make mistakes. Chris agreed to help me learn to use the Let Me Learn Process Advanced Learning System to plan repurpose training that was going to be required to achieve the organization's goal of retooling its labor force.

At the plant, the process was introduced first to the staff and then to all employees, giving us a common language to use when discussing our learning. Individuals were able to identify the approaches to learning that worked best for them and communicate that effectively to others around them. The experiment lasted approximately one year. In addition to completing the job transitions without any quality incidents and with all batches shipping on time, we experienced less conflict among the staff and improved teamwork throughout the plant.

The results of this experience convinced me that the Let Me Learn Process could be a powerful force in corporate America. Not only does it provide a common language that makes it easier for managers and subordinates to discuss and implement specific individual development plans, but it also provides tools that are simple to understand and easy to apply to Decoding specific tasks and to developing strategies to fit individual learning approaches to accomplishing the task.

This experience had a profound impact on me personally. I have always been an enthusiastic learner and worked hard to develop the people who worked for me. But before being introduced to the Let Me Learn Process, I assumed that most people learned pretty much the same way I did. Although I had been very successful in helping some of my employees develop their skills and capabilities, I had struggled with others. The Let Me Learn Process helped me both to understand myself as a learner and to recognize and accept the approaches taken by others, greatly improving the effectiveness of my coaching and guidance.

A Final Word of Encouragement

I believe that in today's global business environment, the companies that are best able to navigate the competitive and often confusing economic challenges facing them will be those with the ability to learn quickly and the flexibility to change course nimbly when it is required. If you are interested in becoming a more flexible, adaptable, and successful person, then understanding yourself as a learner is crucial. *Finding Your Way: Navigating Life by Understanding Your Learning Self* will give you both insight into your unique approach to learning and the tools required to take that knowledge and translate it into greater achievement at work.

Noreen C. Campbell

FINDING YOUR WAY

Acknowledgments

Acknowledgments

There are a number of people who have helped me find my way in life: my parents whose spiritual nurturing led me to find my True North, my husband and dearest friend, Dale, who has kept me on course when work and life circumstances sought to compromise my True North and diminish the use of my Compass Rose, and Bob Kottkamp, who first took me sailing and then helped me explore how understanding learning can make a difference for a lifetime.

INTRODUCTION

"But I Didn't Know I Was Lost!"

Have you ever been lost? In this day and age, it may strike you as odd for an author to begin a book by asking such a question. With GPSs adorning our dashboards, OnStar just a click away, and MapQuest at our fingertips, how is it possible ever to be lost?

The question posed here is not meant to refer to your geo-position or your physical location. Instead, the question refers to your feelings in a learning setting or work environment.

For example, have you ever felt lost when trying to complete an assigned task? When reading directions for assembling a toy? When participating in a team meeting? How about in a classroom, a lecture hall, or a corporate training room? You start to think to yourself, "I'm getting lost here. I'm not following this. How am I supposed to wrap my mind around this? Am I the only one who does not understand this stuff?"

Or maybe you felt lost when your project supervisor or course instructor asked you to write a brief summary of your most recent team meeting, and you felt like doing anything to avoid the dreaded writing task. Maybe the word "brief" made you nervous or uncomfortable.

You might have said to yourself, "That was a very important session we just completed. Brief won't do the job. The folks who weren't here will really be left out of the loop if they don't receive a blow-by-blow account of what transpired. How am I going to be brief *and* thorough?"

Or worse yet, within 30 minutes of receiving the assignment, you might have sat down, cranked out the summary, and e-mailed it. Then later that afternoon, you received an e-mail saying that your supervisor had rethought the brief summary and wanted a more thorough account of the meeting, including graphs and charts. Your frustration over the change in directions required you to pop an antacid.

Or maybe this was the scenario: You sat in a conference room with your team members as you were receiving directions about a new team project. You tried to be patient, but the time was drawing short, and you could no longer hold in your frustration. You knew what the task required. You understood it from the start of the briefing.

You understood the concept. In fact, you *got it* long before the end of the explanation. But your teammates didn't.

Why did they keep asking for more, and more, and more, details? Inside, you said repeatedly, "All right already. Let's move on!"

Then, out of frustration or boredom, you allowed your mind to move into another more interesting set of problems—only to be pulled back to reality when the person in charge of the training session called on you. "Not now!" you screamed inside your head. You had no idea what question you had been asked. Your colleagues stared at you in anticipation. This was your golden opportunity to shine, and you blew it. And how did you feel? Angry? Misunderstood? Unappreciated? It's not always easy to find your way in a boardroom or a classroom.

Lost—But Not Willing to Ask for Directions?

Truly, finding your way as a learner is a major challenge in life. The purpose of *Finding Your Way: Navigating Life by Understanding Your Learning Self* is to help you meet that challenge. The goals of *Finding Your Way* are to help you understand why you sometimes feel lost, and to equip you to achieve greater success and fulfillment in your personal and professional life by providing you with effective learning tools.

Do I Really Need to Find My Way?

The intended audience for this book is quite varied. Some individuals may have been stellar students who seek to enhance their learning skills. After all, what is the well-known corporate adage?

"Chance favors the prepared mind."
—Louis Pasteur

Some intended readers may be adults who struggled in school and remain bewildered and haunted by those experiences, fearful of reentering the world of continuing education. Others may have hated school, endured it as a necessary evil, but who, having survived that dreadful experience, soared as problem solvers and entrepreneurs in the arena of life. These readers will find in these pages a reasonable explanation for what may have seemed like a contradiction in their lives. In fact, the pattern of failure in school and success in life is quite common—and if you read on, you'll discover why.

This book is written especially for those who are still searching for a way to make learning work for them; those who are unsatisfied with their work performance; and those who seek greater self understanding to change, grow, and achieve better results.

Finally, this book is written for the corporate trainers, instructors, and teachers who want to reach more of their trainees and students.

A Guide to Navigating the Text

Finding Your Way is structured to guide you on a very interactive and personal journey. You will discover how to use your mind with intention—that is, with a consciousness of what you are doing and why you are doing it—to absorb information and develop skills and judgment through self-directed assessment and personal reflection. Throughout the book, you will be introduced to a new vocabulary that allows you to express yourself in specific terms as you learn to navigate life using your Directional Learning Forces or Learning Processes (See Glossary). You will note that throughout the text the words, Learning Patterns, Learning Processes, Directional Forces, and Directional Learning Processes, are used interchangeably.

Each chapter begins with a bulleted focus statement followed by The Story, which brings the focus of the bulleted statement into your personal life context. It is followed by The Learning, an extension of the focus that addresses various aspects of your personal learning journey and guides you to use the directional tools appropriately in your life.

All chapters include a review of the chapter's key ideas called, Boxing the Compass, followed by Taking Stock activities intended to extend the "aha moments" that have occurred as you interacted with the ideas and information contained in the chapter—that is, as you learned. Finally, space for you to record Insights is provided at the end of each chapter.

Each of the activities encourages you to implement the insights gained from the chapter. After all, having begun a personal learning journey that results in significant learning outcomes, why would you not want to share the defining experience with others who are part of your varied learning environments—people in your training rooms, classrooms, and, yes, living room!

Finding Your Way: Navigating Life by Understanding Your Learning Self gives you a chance to affirm yourself as a learner *regardless of your age or stage in life*. Most important, it guides your journey to achieve success in the myriad of life's central issues: school, career, relationships, and work. Read these pages, do the suggested activities, and allow yourself to continue your learning journey. Gain a richer perspective as you explore your stated True North, your established destination, and your new level of self-awareness provided by the Compass Rose of your Learning Processes.

Part I

Finding Your Way:
Setting the Course

1. EXAMINING THE COORDINATES IN YOUR LIFE

"It is a sad fate for a man to die too
well known to everybody else, and still
unknown to himself."

—Sir Francis Bacon

The Focus

- Understanding the importance of your True North
- Examining your personal learning story

Ancient astronomers and mariners used to stare at the night sky and glory in its magnitude and beauty. They also gloried in the night sky for another reason. More than just a canopy of wonder and beauty, the night sky served a vital purpose for them: It was the only means for finding their way. Until the development of more modern technology, the North Star and pole stars in the Northern and Southern Hemispheres respectively, were the central reference points for all navigation.

Today, we stare at that same night sky and glory in its beauty, but few of us would see it as a means for finding our way. Yet the evening sky does hold for us a metaphorical significance: Embedded within each of us lies our North Star, our Southern Cross, our figurative reference point that helps us find our way.

Just as the mariners of old were carefully schooled in their knowledge of the North Star and the Southern Cross, this chapter encourages you to study your personal universe, identifying the Polaris or the purpose of your life, which we refer to as your True North. After all, if you intend to arrive at the life goal you have set for yourself, your chosen destination, then it is important for you to consider what your True North is. What is the guiding and most trustworthy point of reference that directs your life? What attracts your attention and focuses your passion for learning and living?

More than identifying your True North, this chapter seeks to engage you in identifying how you have *learned* and used your True North throughout your life. In other words, what experiences did you have that shaped and molded your perspective on life and resulted in what you have chosen to value as central to your life? After all, your True North is not something you chose randomly, but something you repeatedly found merit and joy in understanding and developing. To recognize the significance of your life's True North, you will want to revisit the learning experiences that shaped and molded it. Here is what I learned when I revisited my personal learning journey.

The Story

My Learning Journey

I was raised in Northern Wisconsin by a loving mother and father who adopted me when they were 36 and 41 respectively. These dear people of faith caringly loved and nurtured me but were often bewildered by my behavior and learning habits. My mother, at one time a legal secretary, kept copious records and a very well-organized household. My father, an electrical engineer and church musician, dutifully sought to rein in my free spirit whenever he thought I was setting myself up for failure or embarrassment.

Meanwhile, my mother "schooled" me in how to organize my room, develop a weekly dinner menu, and maintain a household of which the Homemakers of America would be proud. Blessedly, my parents appreciated my idea of turning my bedroom closet into a newspaper office. They smiled proudly when I published my first story, consisting of my hand-printed sentences interwoven with pictures cut from Christmas cards and nested in balls of cotton glued on tin foil. They drew the line, however, when at age five, I went out on my first reporting venture, which involved me walking the shoulder of a busy highway to find my brother, who was attending grade school almost two miles away!

Thankfully, they did not judge me or punish me for the apparent differences we had, but instead they sought to accommodate my unique perspective on learning and living while refining my social graces to fit the more staid, conventional culture in which I was being raised.

I began my formal schooling in a renovated two-room chicken coop, which suited me just fine. I thrived on listening to the teacher and students of the other three grades who occupied my classroom. I was never bored because there were too many things going on to keep me occupied. I reveled in the myriad of activities I could watch or do on my own. My idea bank grew and grew with every passing week.

After my elementary years, I was sent to a large regional junior-senior high where I soon recognized that "kids from the country" were not expected to excel. But I did. Early on, I staked out where I could succeed (debate and forensics), set goals for what I wanted to achieve during my four years of high school (recognition for a unique accomplishment), and began to break the mold of others' expectations of me. By this time, you may have surmised that breaking the mold by bringing unique ideas to the table appears to be the repeated theme of my learning journey, and it is. But often, my ideas were not well received.

For example, I had a geometry teacher who was new to teaching. He was determined to do what most first-year teachers do—get a handle on classroom management. Unfortunately, he went a bit overboard. He required that if we arrived late to class for any reason, we were to stand the remainder of the class period at our desk. I convinced my fellow college-prep classmates to "boycott the bell" by standing outside the door until the period bell had rung and then enter the classroom. We then stood as a group for the next 55 minutes.

The young geometry teacher, who was short of stature, soon found himself staring up at his students! He realized that his rule had created more problems than solutions for him, and he grudgingly discontinued the rule, but not without first noting who had led the insurrection.

When I entered college, I brought my breaking-the-mold learning behaviors with me. In Comp I class, I simply took each assignment carefully described in the syllabus, twisted it until I was comfortable with it, and then wrote what I wanted to write. I had no idea how to "decode" the meaning of the writing assignment. I had no idea where the professor was coming from and that what was assigned was done with a specific intent. I didn't see the plan, the purpose of it. Besides, I thought I had a *better* idea for the assignment. So off I went, breaking the mold of the syllabus to create a match between how I learned and the task at hand.

I graduated from college three years to the day I graduated from high school. I had learned lots of "stuff" but nothing that would help me navigate life. Looking back, I recognize now what I did not understand then: I let ideas rule my life. Different, scattered, mentally playful, full of risk taking, unbounded—that is who I was, and to a great degree, still am. These behaviors manifested themselves in my life throughout school, college, and my several careers in planning, teaching, and consulting.

For many years, I was not able to understand why I did what I did or saw the world as I did. I was simply aware that as a student, teacher, trainer, urban planner, union organizer, curriculum coordinator, consultant, and professor, I walked, hopped, and danced to the proverbial sound of the different drummer and played my own 76 trombones! Thankfully, however, my learning journey did not end at that point.

The Learning

It took me 20 years, two more degrees, and four professions later to recognize that I could unravel the enigma I was to myself and others.

The insights that helped me to be able to direct my actions to achieve my True North were slow in coming. I fought the need to slow down and dig deeply. (I completed my master's degree in urban planning in 15 months and my doctorate in educational leadership in three years.) I needed to consider what it is about rules that raises my ire and what it is about ideas that lights my fire! Painfully, I had to confront the fact that getting a high from ideas or always seeking the fastest way to get things done had cheated me out of a true sense of myself and my capacity. It limited my potential to become what I set out to be in life: an effective teacher of others.

It has only been in the past 15 years that I have come to grips with the fact that my learning behaviors are identical to my teaching and leading behaviors. I taught content, initiated programs, and took on new ventures without ever understanding what was directing me. I never invested in understanding how to bring others along with my thinking and my ways of doing things. I was not helping others learn what I was trying to teach them. I was imposing on them my way of "taking in the world around me and making sense of it" (a definition I coined 10 years ago, to describe learning in the context of the real world, not the classroom) without equipping them to use *their* learning journey to digest what I was feeding them in a manner that worked for me but not for *them*.

A review of my journey brought me to the stark realization that while I was leading some people, I was ignoring and denying others. Those, who learned as I did, felt successful and rewarded under my tutelage and leadership, while those who learned differently were undernourished or confused. They felt, I am certain, left behind in the dust of "hurry up," "please me," "take risks," "quit asking so many questions," and "just take this and make your own way." In other words, I was not helping them to find their way. I was not helping them to understand their learning selves. I was not coaching them to examine their experiences and to see the consistency or inconsistency of their choices. I was not helping them find a sense of their True North nor directing their actions to achieve it. I actually impeded their ability to find their way by not encouraging them to reflect on their learning experiences because I had not taken the time to reflect on my own.

The Learning Journey:
The Demarcation of Your True North

A review of your personal learning journey leads you to understand your learning self in a way rarely explored in formal education or in the work world. Because we often fail to take this journey, our potential lies dormant—undiscovered, unexplored, and undeveloped.

There are two primary reasons this occurs. First, we fail as individuals to recognize that we *have* a purpose. Early on, we are subsumed in an educational culture that sees us only as test scores, a diploma, a certification, or a label. Lost in this fog, we fail to reach toward our Polaris, to focus on who we are and what we can become.

The second reason we don't achieve our potential is that we don't know how to navigate our lives to achieve success. Instead, we strive, we struggle, and we experience mistakes, but we do not grow from them. Lacking an understanding of our learning journey, we repeat our mistakes, failing to navigate our lives' purposes. That brings me to what I hope will emerge for you as the central message of this book: *Within each of us is a striving that reveals our potential, our purpose—our True North*. Also within each of us is a set of directional tools, Learning Processes that we can use with the skill of a navigator, to "set a course, stay the course, and come safe home," having achieved our True North.

We are not the first people who have sought the best means for finding our way. I am certain that it has been true throughout history: Men and women have striven to achieve their utmost potential. What have been the tools they have used to achieve this success? I would suggest it is their Learning Processes—their Mental Operations used in concert with their innate human capacities. It is the joining of our intellectual potential, in its multiple forms, with our mental operations that equips us to take in the world around us and make sense of it. Women, men, and children all possess these Processes and use them to make their lives work.

But how well do they use them? How well do *you* use your Learning Processes? How prepared are you to set your life course by using your learning tools? How prepared are you to adapt, overcome, and succeed?

Tom Friedman's, *The World Is Flat* (2005), assures us that geopositioning ourselves for this century clearly requires us to use every resource in our grasp to be able to achieve our life goals. More than maps and sextants, more than high-tech gadgets, more than an understanding of the laws of physics, we need an understanding of ourselves to be able to navigate our life potential.

My Learning Journey Revisited

Looking back at my life, I recognize that my learning journey often was at odds with the learning situations in which I found myself. I was the one whose ideas were askew or inconsistent with those of the people around me at home, in school, or at work. Underlying it all was the fact that I never felt valued or accepted for who I was.

Because I felt that I was a bit of an outsider, I was always empathetic with those who found themselves not fitting in, whether in the classroom or in the workplace. I cared about what they were experiencing, and I wanted them to feel valued.

But only in recent years have I discovered how to help them—
and myself.

After 60 years, I have found a sense of fulfillment as I continue on my personal learning journey. This sense comes from
having identified my True North, my purpose in life—to help
people whose sense of self as learners is unrecognized, underval-
ued, or underused.

This book is my attempt to share with you how you, too,
can find your way and gain an awareness of your purpose by ex-
ploring your learning journey. If it achieves its purpose, it will
help you recognize your True North, identify the power of your
Learning Processes, and apply that knowledge to achieve safe
harbor, having achieved the desires of your heart.

Boxing the Compass

- Recognizing the central role of your personal learning
  story helps you identify your True North and set the
  course for navigating your life.
- Understanding the importance of your personal
  Learning Processes is central to all of your life's journey.

Taking Stock

Can you identify your True North? Jot down words or
sketch something that represents your True North. How well
have you used your True North to guide you in your choices in
school, work, and your personal life?

Think about your learning journey.

- If you had to chart your journey, what would your map look like?
- Where were the critical stopping points? Where were the high and low points in the journey?
- List the five most important stops you have made along your life journey.
- If you had to create a road sign for each stop, what would it look like?
- How do these signs relate to your True North?

Insights

Record Your Insights here:

2. RECOGNIZING THE IMPORTANCE OF YOUR COMPASS ROSE

"Taking charge of your own learning is
part of taking charge of your own life."

—Warren Bennis
On Becoming a Leader

The Focus

- Understanding the concept of the Compass Rose
- Identifying the directional tools of the mind

The Compass Rose represents a concept of navigation and exploration that dates back to the early 12th century. Its purpose was to indicate the direction of the ocean's winds (32 in number), thereby allowing navigators to harness the various winds to power their passage across the seas.

Today's maps bear little resemblance to the intricacy and beauty of the cartographer's rendering of a Compass Rose centuries ago. Yet I am intrigued with the image of a Compass Rose because it speaks to me in a metaphorical manner of our need to have sound navigational tools to find our way in life.

To anticipate and take advantage of the winds of change that come into our lives, we need specific directional tools that can help us plot our course. Further, as we seek to plot our course, it is vital that we have a guide that identifies and explains the Directional Forces that we will encounter and that help us arrive safely at our destination. What is it that each of us possesses that forms our personal Compass Rose?

When Albert Einstein was four or five years old and first gazed upon a compass, he was intrigued. He was especially fascinated by, as he later recalled, "its determination." Many years later, he told of this experience and marked it as the moment when he realized that "there must be something deeply hidden behind everything" (Schilpp, 1979).

Einstein said:

> Why do we come, sometimes spontaneously, to wonder about something? I think that wondering to one's self occurs when an experience

conflicts with our fixed ways of seeing the
world. I had one such experience of wondering
when I was a child of four or five and my father
showed me a compass. This needle behaved
in such a determined way and did not fit into
the usual explanation of how the world works.
That is that you must touch something to move
it. I still remember now, or I believe that I remember, that this experience made a deep and
lasting impression on me. There must be something deeply hidden behind everything (p. 9).

I would suggest that each of us has Directional Forces that
lie deeply hidden in our brain-mind connection that drive our
approach to learning. These "winds" determine our direction
for learning and form our internal Compass Rose. If we allow
them to remain undiscovered and unfettered, then we travel at
their behest, and we are buffeted from one position to another,
one career to another, one relationship to another without ever
determining our current position or plotting a way to reach our
destination.

To understand our learning selves is to set ourselves on a
course of self-awareness and preparedness as no other single
piece of knowledge can. In Chapter 1, we identified the cen-
trality of our True North to the course of our lives. This chapter
continues that message, pointing out that each of us must grab
hold of our Learning Processes and understand the directional
tool they can be for achieving our True North.

The Story

I would like to introduce you to a man who changed the course of history by persisting in solving a problem that had escaped solution for centuries. The problem? How to determine longitude. According to Dava Sobel (1996), author of *Longitude: The True Story of the Lone Genius Who Solved the Greatest Scientific Problem of His Time*, "Many thousands of lives had been lost at sea over the centuries due to the inability to determine an east-west position when, in 1714, the British Parliament offered a king's ransom of £20 million to anyone who could solve the problem of how to measure longitude at sea." The man who rose to meet this enormous challenge was a little-known clockmaker, John Harrison.

In terms of information, there is little I can add to the story of Harrison so thoughtfully and eloquently told by Sobel (1996) except to add that after many years of frustration, he did realize the prize for which he had striven. Summarized, John Harrison, clock smith and inventor, devised the chronometer, which allowed longitude to be measured and, thereby, made it possible to plot a navigational course that was much more refined and accurate. His invention literally changed the course of commerce, saving hundreds of sailors' lives and propelling the future of the British Commonwealth forward to the acme it achieved through its maritime commerce.

Although I have little content to add to his story, I can comment on the pain and frustration this man experienced throughout his life because of his lack of awareness of his internal Compass Rose of Learning Processes.

To revisit Einstein's comment, "Deeply hidden behind everything" lay the fact that Harrison's mind operated with such precision and detail that he was unable to organize, edit, and articulate his thoughts in a manner that was lucid and comprehensible to others.

Because his formal education was very limited, he was considered by members of the Royal Observatory to be a bit of a dolt; he could not articulate either orally or in writing the theory behind his groundbreaking invention. He could build, but he could not explain!

So significant was his inability to communicate in a coherent manner that the governors of the Royal Observatory actually refused to believe that he had invented the chronometer. They hammered it into bits, saying, "If you did indeed build this, then you can build it again." The totality of his scientific writings suffered from the same problem. In one of his treatises, a single sentence went on for no less than five pages! In 1775, when he was 82, he wrote an account of his life's work. He entitled his book, *A Description Concerning Such Mechanism As Will Afford a Nice, or True Mensuration of Time; Together With Some Account of the Attempts for the Discovery of the Longitude by the Moon: As Also An Account of the Discovery of the Scale of Music, by John Harrison, Inventor of the Time-Keeper For The Longitude At Sea.* John Harrison, unaware of his internal Compass Rose of Learning Processes, became the victim of them. Herein lies the irony!

Harrison's True North lay in his determination to solve a problem whose solution evaded the most erudite minds of his time. His learning processes consisted of his powers of observation, his doggedness to find solutions, and his workmanship.

Yet Harrison's Compass Rose of learning tools, the very thing that powered his genius, separated him from others, provided him with years of frustration, and left him diminished in spirit and professional stature. Harrison, who worked his entire life to solve the most challenging problem of sea navigation, landed personally on the rocky shoals of failed communication, preventing him from achieving in his lifetime the prominence and success he was rightfully due. Years later, the British historian Thomas Babington Macaulay would write of him, "[He was a] great man with the wisdom to devise and the courage to perform that which he lacked the language to explain" (Smiles, 1884).

The Learning

Like Harrison, we seek to be listened to and understood. We articulate our thoughts and look to others to grasp our meaning. We plan or not, crave information or not, problem solve or not, and revel in cutting-edge ideas or not. By now, I am certain you have picked up on the cadence of the previous sentence. If you did, then you are becoming aware of the central importance of the "we do or we do not" to our Learning Processes. When we can identify our Learning Processes to navigate our lives, then we can use our Directional Forces to succeed and achieve.

John Harrison and You

"But I'm not a John Harrison," you're saying. You would never think of trying to solve a problem as sophisticated or farreaching as the one he confronted. Maybe you are a manager for UPS or a preschool teacher, a computer programmer, or someone starting at the bottom of the corporate ladder. Maybe you aspire to a more complete life, a more satisfying career, or better relationships with coworkers, friends, or family members.

Gregory's Journey (Dr. Gregory Dunham)

Maybe your situation is much like that of someone I know: Gregory is a high school principal who was raised in the Boston area. Greg's mother nurtured his interest in academics and kept a tight rein on him until he completed high school and entered college, where he majored in engineering. His school counselor suggested he do so because of Greg's mathematical abilities. Four years later, Greg found himself employed but very unhappy. Engineering clearly wasn't his thing.

He wrote:

> I actually began my professional life as a research and development engineer for a transistor company. This company grew silicone chips, a process of manufacturing and assembling transistors for use in miniature amplifiers. I enjoyed the prestige of this career but soon began to feel isolated, having no meaningful interaction with people during my working hours. My fondest memories of that company were during lunch, when the entire research unit ate together, and we told stories and shared experiences.
>
> After a while, I began to wonder why and how I chose this profession as my career. I reflected

back to my high school days. I was always a very good math student, and one day my guidance counselor asked, "Gregory, what do you want to do when you graduate from high school?" I had no idea.

She said, "You know, with your math aptitude you could be an engineer." It sounded good to me. When I told my parents that I wanted to be an engineer, they were pleased. When I told my friends that I was going to be an engineer, they were impressed. The interesting thing about that decision is that it was totally based on one aspect of what I did well, but it did not take into consideration what provided me with a professional goal, a sense of focus, or an awareness of how to achieve success. Within a few years of entering that profession, I changed careers and took my math skills into secondary education, and I became a high school math teacher.

It was not until many years later, having achieved the position of high school principal, that I became aware of how it was possible to have been so mismatched with my first career: My high school counselor had no real basis on which to help me select an appropriate career because she had no idea who I was beyond my record of grades and activities. My awareness of what went wrong back then was truly cathartic for me.

For years, I wondered why I did not find engineering energizing, but I loved teaching math. As I spent time looking back on my learning journey, examining it vis-á-vis my knowledge of my learning self, it became very clear: I was good in math because I had an innate mathematical intelligence, which I processed by asking questions until I understood. I also learned by being allowed to see things in more than one way and take some risks. This helped me particularly with geometry. Yet I still needed to understand why engineering was not energizing to me, a person who had a strong math aptitude.

I found the explanation by examining my Learning Processes, my Compass Rose. I did not find fulfillment in an engineering career because I did not have a natural curiosity about how things worked—a prime tenet for a good engineer! I had little technical curiosity.

If my guidance counselor had known my Learning Processes, she could have made more informed recommendations to me regarding my future. More important, if I had knowledge of the Learning Forces that made up my Compass Rose,

I could have had more control over my choices
and could have made them with more intention.

Three careers and many years later, Dr. Gregory Dunham
finally *found his way*. Like Gregory, unless you understand the
composition of your internal Compass Rose, you will survive
by chance and intuition, not succeed and achieve through conscious planning and focused effort.

The Price of Being Compass-Less

Just like John Harrison and Gregory Dunham, millions
of people possess the innate ability and talent to succeed, but
they do not know how to use their Directional Forces for learning or leading others. Many people go through life with an
intuitive sense of their Compass Rose, but fail to use their
internal Directional Learning Forces to achieve their desired
outcomes.

One only needs to open the sports pages to find athletes
who make it to the big leagues and then find their careers stall.
They never reach the "superstar" level that had been predicted
for them. Or coaches who take their team to the brink of success
year after year but never win a championship—failing repeatedly because they don't know the composition of their personal
Compass Rose or that of team members and assistant coaches.
What about the EMT captain who doesn't know the Learning
Compass of his men and women?

Or bringing the phenomenon closer to home, what happens if you are promoted to the position that has been your

lifelong dream, and suddenly, all of the means you used to achieve this success are no longer working for you? Did your True North change? Did you leave your Compass Rose behind? Or had you always navigated life in one way and now that you find yourself sailing different seas, you had no Directional Forces to guide you? Did you find that those things that you used intuitively before were not working effectively anymore? That's when it dawns on you: Knowing the composition of your Compass Rose, your Directional Forces, is the key to bringing your human potential to fruition.

Finding Your Way: Identifying Your Compass Rose

Identifying your Compass Rose begins by collecting data about yourself—how you think, what actions you take as a result, and what your emotions respond to in different situations. Almost 15 years ago, a colleague and I developed a means to gather that information and interpret it in a valid and reliable manner. You can find a specially designed version of that instrument, the Learning Connections Inventory (LCI), in Appendix A. Using the directions provided under Taking Stock at the conclusion of this chapter, complete the survey and gain a more complete representation of the Compass Rose of your Learning Processes

Here is your opportunity to begin to develop your Compass Rose using the information you have gathered about your learning self. The development of your personal Compass Rose will mark the beginning of your new venture in finding your way.

Boxing the Compass

- Learning Processes provide a powerful insight into your communication with others as well as an understanding of yourself. There's little use having a True North if you don't have the navigational tools to help you reach your destination.
- Understanding the direction of your Learning Processes provides a powerful insight into your communication with others as well as an understanding of yourself.

Taking Stock

- Complete the Learning Connections Inventory. (See Appendix A.)
- This is a survey of your individual Learning Processes. You are the expert when it comes to answering these questions.
- You can begin with Part I (Questions 1 through 28 require you to record your reaction to a series of statements about learning on a continuum of 1 to 5), or you can begin with Part II (three questions that require you to write short answers). Take your time and enjoy doing both parts.
- Before you begin Part I, take a moment to write your definition for each of the choices you have on the continuum. What is an "Always" for you? A "Never"? An "Almost Always" (daily with few exceptions)? An "Almost Never" (once a year)?

- Avoid using "Sometimes" as your answer *unless* the answer truly is sometimes. Don't use "Sometimes" as your answer when you can't decide what the answer should be. Instead, stop and think. Is this something I do a few times a month?
- Be honest!
- Note that you are free to tweak a word or phrase within a given question if you feel changing the wording will help you respond with a more accurate choice on the continuum.
- When you have finished answering both Parts I and II, read the directions for scoring the LCI, which are printed at the top of the scoring sheet. Once you have completed the scoring sheet, fill in the graph, return to this chapter, and enter your LCI Scale Scores in the boxes that match the scale categories: Sequence, Precision, Technical Reasoning, and Confluence, located on the blank Compass Rose. (See Figure 2.2.)

Figure 2.2 Personal Compass Rose

Insights

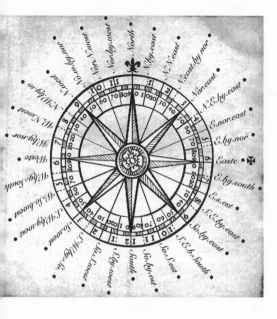

3. BOXING YOUR COMPASS ROSE

> "Real learning gets to the heart of
> what it means to be human."
>
> —Peter Senge
> *The Fifth Discipline*

The Focus

- Understanding learning as a tool for navigating your life
- Understanding how our learning affects our leading

The word "learning" usually evokes a variety of responses from people. Most equate learning with school. That's because in most cultures school is a proxy for learning. Actually, being a student is an even closer match. But those of us who haven't been in a school for years know that learning isn't confined to a formal school setting. In fact, we were doing lots of learning long before we ever entered the schoolyard gate and have continued learning long after we left the confines of the formal classroom. To lose sight of the fact that learning takes place outside of school, and sometimes even in spite of school, is to miss the central role learning plays in our lives.

Learning is the center of our human essence. Learning directs our thoughts, our actions, and our feelings. It gives us a sense of being; it enables us to function, to grow in understanding, and to change deliberately. Here I am speaking of the learning that occurs when our senses take in the world around us and respond to it. Stimuli (sight, sound, touch, taste, and smell) are constantly bombarding us. Just look at the neon signs, the video players in our cars, or the MP3 players adorning our children's heads. We are surrounded by stimuli! How we handle the stimuli reflects how we learn.

You see, once stimuli enter our brain-mind system, we proceed to filter, sort and sift, and process it to both respond to it appropriately as well as store it for later retrieval. *How* we each, individually, do these actions is what makes us different as learners. These differences are reflected in our Learning Processes and in our Compass Roses.

There is no doubt about it; *how* we learn makes a difference in our lives. Consequently, we need to become very familiar with how we learn and what makes up our internal Directional Forces. Clearly, if we intend to navigate our lives well, if we intend to "set our course, stay the course, and come safe home," then we need to know how we learn and how to use our Directional Learning Forces to navigate our lives and steer the course we have set. Beyond any doubt, understanding our Learning Processes is the next step to finding our way.

The Story

The Brain-Mind Connection

Earlier, I referred to learning as interacting with the world around us. Learning requires the use of our senses to take in various stimuli, and it requires the brain to channel, connect, and respond to sensory stimuli, but learning also involves the mind—which is more than the machinery that sits atop our shoulders. Our minds go far beyond the physiological limitations of our gray matter.

What follows is a simple representation of that extremely complex operation. Read it for insight and understanding, not as a detailed science text. (See Figure 3.2.)

Learning—it all begins with our senses. Our ears, eyes, nose, skin, and tongue serve as the first line of receptors that initiate learning. They gather and channel stimuli into the brain, which channels it through its complex series of regions and its neuron circuitry. No doubt about it, Einstein was correct when he referred to the mind as the greatest complexity in the universe. In the brain's electrochemical processing, the stimulus is "handled" by a number of operations, ultimately moving to a higher level of mental processing (the mind). There it is filtered by our individual Learning Processes, (i.e., either blocked, welcomed, or given limited access to continue on its way to operate within our mind and memory). The stimuli that make it through the brain-mind interface are then translated into symbols and passed to our working memory to become a part of our consciousness (declarative memory) or subconsciousness (nondeclarative memory).

Figure 3.2 Brain-Mind Connection

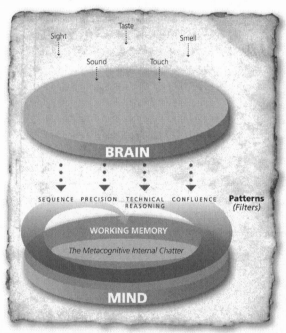

I believe that our Learning Processes, our Compass Rose, lie (figuratively) at the juncture where stimuli morph from electrochemical gibberish into symbolic representation (oral and written language, numbers, musical notes, etc.). Acting as a sort-and-sift filtering mechanism, our Patterned Processes serve to limit or welcome an individual stimulus as it is being shaped, translated, and directed by our working memory into any number of memory channels where it is stored for later retrieval and use.

The Learning

The Compass Rose of Our Learning

The Compass Rose of our learning, that is, our set of navigational directional tools, directs the way that each of us learns. The manner in which we learn is different from our intelligences, which are genetically based and consist of our unique talents, such as mathematical ability, athletic ability, artistic ability, and the like, and our personality, which also has genetic ties to our family tree through its taproot of temperament. Unlike these genetically endowed traits, the way we learn is the result of what the best science suggests is the outcome of our brain-mind circuitry as it seeks a unity, a wholeness, a predictability. As Sherwin Nuland (2007) of Yale said, our brain-mind connection forms "a rhythm and harmony of operation, selecting the cells it values, favoring those that create a unity, and shunning those that give a sense of chaos."

As we reflect on the Directional Forces of our Compass Rose (i.e., the Learning Processes that operate in our minds), we recognize the central unifying role these processes play in forming and operating our learning system. To put this very important information into a more familiar context, consider the following examples of how our Learning Processes manifest themselves in our daily life.

Scenario 1

You sit at a board meeting, using your laptop to record co-pious notes. You look around you and wonder, "Why is Gina studying the agenda so closely instead of recording what is being said? And what is Sam doing adjusting his watchband, fiddling with his PDA, and popping his knuckles? Grow up and pay attention, boy! Does he think he can memorize all this? And then there's Aldridge. I swear if he interrupts the flow of the presentation one more time with his 'alternative' idea, I'm going to spike his mocha latte with something. What is it with this crew? It's obvious no one will know anything about what is being said when the meeting is over—except me, of course, because *I* took the notes. But then again, if I didn't have my fingers recording what was happening, I'd feel like a fish out of water. If it weren't for me, where would our business team be? Right?"

Scenario 2

Three people, standing in the same location, observe a car accident, a minor fender-bender. Each is asked to tell what he or she saw.

Person A says, "I was standing approximately 20-feet away, waiting for the 7:35 bus to take me uptown. I know what time it was because I had just looked at my watch and was wondering why the bus was running late. Then this late-model, blue Chevy just came out of nowhere and broadsided the tan Camry that was waiting to turn left on the arrow. The young man in the Chevy—I'd guess no more than 20 years of age and similar to my son in height and weight who just turned 20 last week—jumped out of his car and began to yell, "Look what you've done now!" at the young mother. Well I assume she was a mother because she had a crumpled child safety seat in her backseat—thank heavens there wasn't a child in it."

Person B reports, "First, this car came up really fast, then it tried to brake but couldn't, so it skidded and slammed into the other car that was in the left turn lane. I looked to see if anyone was hurt. The next thing I knew, a fellow from the first car was yelling, and a woman from the car that was hit was crying. Shortly after that, you folks arrived. Since you are on the scene now, can I leave so I won't be late for my appointment?"

Person C reports, "The one car rear-ended the other. Happens all the time at this intersection. No big deal. Can I go now?"

Scenario 3

You have just seen your child's report card. It isn't good. What's going on? You were an excellent student. Almost all A's throughout high school, a few B's and C's in college, but you nailed all your graduate courses. And even if you attributed the kid's performance to your spouse, you would still say that the child comes from a real good gene pool.

You know the child is "bright." Picks up on things quickly. Doesn't miss a thing. Excels at building things. Can figure out the most complex stuff. Doesn't talk a lot, but gets along well with the rest of the family; however, now that you think about it, she does like to be alone a lot too.

You can't dodge this because not only did you receive the report card but also, in the same mail, you found a letter from the school district's child study team. They want to test your child for possible learning disabilities.

"My child! This can't be happening. Okay, I'll ground that sixth grader so fast. I'll take away computer and TV privileges. No more outdoor play until the grades come up. I'll go to the library and get some books to help her boost the social studies grade. I know now that I need to check the homework more often.

"If the kid reads more and learns to write more than those two-word sentences I find in the composition journal, then maybe things will get better. I'll make my child become a real student. No more excuses. Get motivated. That's the message. Stop being lazy and apply yourself. That's what I'll say, and I'll keep repeating it until things improve, even if I have to become a real hound about it. After all, I want what's best for all of us. Maybe I need to find a tutor, too."

The previous scenarios undergird the point that we each take in the world around us differently. We process the same stimuli, but to different degrees and from different perspectives. We cannot escape the fact that how we take in the world around us and deal with it, affects our everyday decisions, behaviors, plans—our lives! This book is about taking control of how you learn, and making it work for you so that you can navigate your daily life, as well as your future.

Taking control of your learning begins with an awareness of yourself. In other words, your journey begins by understanding your Compass Rose of Directional Forces or Learning Processes.

The Directional Forces of Your Compass Rose: Your Learning Processes

Your Compass Rose of personal learning forces is comprised of your four Learning Patterns. This portion of the chapter will introduce you to the Patterns and the internal composition of each (MacLean, 1978; Snow, 1997). Like the Compass Rose of old, which was comprised of 32 distinct winds, your Compass Rose is comprised of four Directional Learning Forces and their subsets. Read the following pages with care, noting which aspects of the four Learning Processes form your Compass Rose.

At the conclusion of the previous chapter, you were encouraged to respond to a set of 28 statements as well as record your answers to three open-ended questions. You then tallied your Learning Connections Inventory (LCI) responses and recorded your results in the outline of the Compass Rose provided. The numbers you recorded under each of four categories (Sequence, Precision, Technical Reasoning, and Confluence) identify the degree to which you use each of four Learning Processes or Directional Learning Forces in your life.

These processes form the port of entry of your mind. They represent the organization, information, problem-solving, and risk-taking thoughts, actions, and feelings that help you navigate life. As in the case of the Compass Rose, your Patterns form a set of winds of various strengths coming from various directions.

In this and the ensuing chapters, you will find an explanation of what your tallied numbers mean. You will also find ways to use your Directional Learning Forces to navigate your life. If you read this chapter carefully and study its illustrations, you will begin to find your way in a manner you may have never before experienced.

Your LCI Scale Scores

Even though you have recorded your Scale Scores at the end of the prior chapter, I would suggest that you record them again on this page to have them in front of you as you read about what each number signifies:

The four Directional Forces of my Compass Rose:
S ___P ___TR ___ C___

Your LCI results appear as four different scores. (See Figure 3.3 Learning Connections Inventory Scale Scores.) As you can see, the range of the LCI Scale Scores is 7 through 35. Notice that there are no 0 scores. The range of the continuum of the scores form three distinct categories: (1) Use First, (2) Use As Needed, and (3) Avoid. Everyone uses each of these Patterns to some degree.

The most important aspect of the scores is that they tell you the *degree* to which you use each Pattern in combination with the others. No single score or group of scores makes you smarter, brighter, more capable, or less capable. Each has equal value when you analyze the totality of your Learning Processes—the Directional Forces of your Compass Rose of Learning.

Begin the analysis of your Learning Processes by comparing your scores to each of the "degree of use" categories.

Figure 3.3 Range of LCI Scale Scores

How many Learning Processes do you use at the Use First level; how many do you Use As Needed; how many do you Avoid?

Examining Your Compass Rose

Now you are ready to examine each of the Patterns individually to see what lies behind these Learning Forces in you. Remember, if you use a Pattern in the Use First range (25 to 35), you can expect to find yourself saying yes to most of the Pattern characteristics listed.

The Patterns that fall within the Use As Needed range (18 to 24) are the ones that you just don't feel an urgency to use. Sometimes, you actually need to wake them up and let them know that you need to use them—*now*! If one or more of your Patterns are Use As Needed, you will find yourself saying, "I agree with *some* of the characteristics and behaviors cited under a specific Pattern category, but not all of them. I don't feel a strong pull to use this Pattern. I can use it when I need to, but it isn't the Directional Force that I am going to use to navigate a learning situation."

If, on the other hand, your score is in the Avoid range (7 to 17), you will find yourself saying, "I truly do not like to use that Pattern. Frankly, I Avoid using it whenever I can. I don't understand it. I don't enjoy it, and I simply don't like it."

What follows is an expanded explanation of each of the Learning Patterns. I hope this information will help you better identify those you Use First, Use As Needed, and Avoid.

The Directional Forces of Your Compass Rose: Your Learning Processes

Please note that each set of Pattern explanations begins with what people think, do, feel, or say if they use that Pattern at the Use First level (LCI Scale Scores 25 to 35). The set of descriptors is followed by a set that describes what people think, do, feel, and say when they truly Avoid that Pattern (LCI Scale Scores 7 to 17).

As you read the following descriptions of the Use First and Avoid levels of each of your Learning Patterns, consider how each pulls you in a different direction, forming the dynamic action of the Directional Forces in you.

If your LCI score for Sequence is between 25 and 35, then the following explanation of Sequence makes a great deal of sense to you. (See Figure 3.4.) If, on the other hand, your score for Sequence is between 7 and 17, you will find the Avoid Sequence descriptions (See Figure 3.5.) will be much more accurate to how you experience the Directional Force of Sequence.

Figure 3.4 Use First Sequence

If You Use Sequence First

How you think	How you do things	How you feel	Your internal self-talk sometimes said aloud
I think in goals, objectives and steps. I think with clarity not clutter. I think in phases—start-up, progress, completion.	I break tasks into steps. I organize my life by keeping a tight schedule. I strive to do a task methodically from beginning to end	I feel secure when I have the steps laid out. I thrive on a well ordered life. I feel a great sense of satisfaction when I finish a task A-Z.	What's the goal for this task? What's the first step? There is a place for everything and everything in its place. Nothing feels better than crossing an item off my to-do list.

Figure 3.5 Avoid Sequence

If You Avoid Sequence

How you think	How you do things	How you feel	Your internal self-talk sometimes said aloud
These directions are too wordy and too lengthy! I did this before. Why repeat it? Why must I wait for directions?	I read as little of the directions as possible. I don't practice and rehearse. I fail to do all the parts of a task leaving some incomplete.	I feel confused by the wording and the order of most directions. I feel frustrated and bored when I am forced to repeat a task. I don't feel bound by the requirements of the task.	Who wrote these directions anyway? What a waste of my time! Who cares how I do this as long as I get it done?

You will note the descriptive characteristics of Precision are formulated both as Use First (See Figure 3.6.) and then as Avoid. (See Figure 3.7.) Be careful to distinguish that Sequence refers to order, rules, planning, and completeness while Precision focuses on the importance of information, accuracy, exactness, and documentation. An example of the distinct difference between the two Directional Forces is a person who uses Precision at the Use First level and gathers so much information and documentation that his office is awash in piles of folders and projects but who does not possess the use of Sequence to be able to organize or locate the information for fast retrievability. Each Directional Force has its own particular descriptors as the remaining figures illustrate.

Figure 3.6 Use First Precision

If You Use Precision First

How you think	How you do things	How you feel	Your internal self-talk sometimes said aloud
I think in information. I think knowing facts means I am smart. I think knowledge is power.	I write things down and document everything. I leave no piece of information unspoken. I research information and check sources.	I feel confident when I have my notes or journal to refer to. I hate being "out of the know." I feel frustrated when incorrect information is accepted as valid.	Before I decide, I need more information. Where did you get that information? What was your source?

It might be tempting to think that those who Avoid Precision cannot do well in the information age, but actually, that is not true. With the availability of information at the touch of Google or many other search engines, those who Avoid Precision can make their world of work operate successfully as long as they are aware of the Directional Force that would lead them to rely on summaries and abstracts instead of delving into the body of facts available for analysis and projections. Read the descriptors of the Avoid Precision Pattern and determine how to avoid the rocky shoals this Pattern may set you upon if you are not alert to its effects on your Compass Rose.

Figure 3.7 Avoid Precision

If You Avoid Precision

How you think	How you do things	How you feel	Your internal self-talk sometimes said aloud
How am I supposed to remember all this stuff? Do I have to read all of this? What am I expected to write down and keep track of?	I don't have specific answers. I skim instead of read details. I take few, if any, notes.	I feel stupid if I don't have the one expected answer. Pages of information make me feel like I am drowning in words. I fear looking unprepared because my notes are so few.	Stop asking me so many questions! Don't expect me to know names and dates! Do I have to read all of this? Is there a DVD I can watch instead?

Yet another Directional Force, Technical Reasoning, adds an additional awareness to your Compass Rose of Learning Processes. Technical Reasoning's uniqueness (See Figure 3.8.) lies in its *thinking, reasoning, making sense or discerning without the use of words* and poses an interesting juxtaposition to Precision, which is the Learning Process of the most words. Your Technical Reasoning has a bit of a Nike ad sense to it, as this Learning Process urges you to "Just do it!" This Learning Process also demands relevance and practicality. Although Technical Reasoning and Precision can work together at the Use First level, the effect of Technical Reasoning on the usually ready flow of information provided by Precision is muted so that only pertinent facts are shared and "information for information's sake" is not shared.

Figure 3.8 Use First Technical Reasoning

If You Use Technical Reasoning First

How you think	How you do things	How you feel	Your internal self-talk sometimes said aloud
What value does this have in the real world? I figure out how something works without using words. I don't want to read a book about it; I want to get my hands on it.	I charge in and solve real problems. I work in my head and then with my hands. I tinker.	I feel frustrated when the task has no real world relevance. I enjoy competing with myself when figuring out how something works. I like the feel of having the right tool to get the job done.	Why am I required to do this? I don't need to talk about it. I already have it figured out. I can't wait to get my hands on this!

Figure 3.9 Avoid Technical Reasoning

If You Avoid Technical Reasoning

How you think	How you do things	How you feel	Your internal self-talk sometimes said aloud
Why should I care how this works? Somebody has to help me figure this out! Why do I have to make something?	I avoid using tools or fixing/repairing things. I talk about it instead of doing it. I rely on reading the directions in order to assemble a project.	I am inept. I feel frustrated because I can't conceptualize the functions involved in solving the issue. I am very comfortable with my words and thoughts—not tools.	I don't care how it runs; I just want it to run! I'm an educated person; I should be able to solve this! Why can't I just talk or write about it?

It should be clear to you by this point that no Directional Force of your Compass Rose operates in isolation from the others. Your Compass Rose consists of the interaction of all four Directional Forces. The final set of descriptions is of Use First Confluence and Avoid Confluence. (See Figure 3.10 and Figure 3.11.) In the case of Use First Confluence, the person who has this level will generate many ideas and want to implement them all. This is a learner who embraces both the big picture and risktaking. Use First Confluence, coupled with Use First Precision, frequently yields an entrepreneurial approach to business and life.

Figure 3.10 Use First Confluence

If You Use Confluence First

How you think	How you do things	How you feel	Your internal self-talk sometimes said aloud
I think to risk is to learn I think outside the box. I connect things that are seemingly unrelated.	I take risks and push the boundaries. I brainstorm. I read over, under, around, and between the lines.	I am not afraid to fail. I feel energized by possibilities that are still in the idea stage. I revel in connecting the dots!	Nothing ventured, nothing gained! I have an idea. No, wait! I have an even better idea! Think Big Picture!

As noted throughout this section on the Directional Forces of Sequence, Precision, Technical Reasoning, and Confluence, your Compass Rose can consist of any combination of the Use First, Avoid, and Use As Needed levels of these Processes. It is fascinating at times to observe Use First Sequence and Use First Confluence competing for your attention and use. When that occurs, you will find yourself having an idea and immediately seeking to organize it to bring it to fruition. On the other hand, you may have an Avoid Sequence connected to Use First Confluence. Then it's helpful to have someone on your team who can model for you some techniques for organizing your Confluence before it becomes chaos! The descriptions of Avoid Confluence (Figure 3.11) explain the tension that can exist among team members or board members whose Compass Roses consist of varying levels of use of Confluence ranging from Use First to Avoid.

Figure 3.11 Avoid Confluence

If You Avoid Confluence

How you think	How you do things	How you feel	Your internal self-talk sometimes said aloud
Has this been well thought out??	I don't take risks without a plan.	I feel unsettled.	Let's not lose sight of the plan. Stay focused!
I hate brainstorming!	I avoid improvising at the last minute.	I feel left out because I can't come up with ideas fast enough.	Where did that idea come from?
Where is this heading?	I can't follow "outside of the box" thinking.	This is out of control! No more changes or surprises, please!	Get a grip!! Let's deal with current realities not fantasies!

You may have identified your Compass Rose by reading through these statements, but you aren't finished "boxing your Compass Rose" until you have checked to see if your scores for Use First or Avoid match your short answers. In other words, are the answers you circled for the 28 questions mirrored by what you wrote for the self-generated short answers? As you read through the scores and the matching written responses, note that not every score has a written response to match it. Usually, you will find a match for one or two Patterns—those that you Use First and those you Avoid. That is the case with both Sample Responses of Dynamic Learner I and II. (See Figure 3.12 and Figure 3.13.)

Figure 3.12 Sample Responses Dynamic Learner I

		What Makes Assignments Frustrating for You?	What Would You Do to Show What You Have Learned?
Sequence Use As Needed	21		
Precision Use First	34	Not having access to info	Write a report
Technical Reasoning Use First	23		
Confluence Avoid	9	When I have to learn a new system, and I don't have enough information to guide me.	

Notice this individual's references to information and writing match the description of Use Precision First (See Figure 3.6.), while the reference to not wanting to learn something new without sufficient information matches both Avoid Confluence (See Figure 3.11.) and Use First Precision. (See Figure 3.6.) In Figure 3.13, you will notice that the written responses contain references to directions and building, two distinct references to the Directional Forces of Sequence and Technical Reasoning respectively.

Figure 3.13 Sample Responses Dynamic Learner II

		What Makes Assignments Frustrating for You?	What Would You Do to Show What You Have Learned?
Sequence Use First	29	If the directions are not given to me clearly.	I would develop a plan and move step-by-step until it's completed.
Precision Use As Needed	22		
Technical Reasoning Use First	25	Nothing. I just do it!	Build a model or pro-totype of the project.
Confluence Use As Needed	23		

Written responses that are equally clear are found in Figure 3.14, where this individual's Compass Rose consists of one Avoid Learning Process (Sequence) and three Use First Learning Processes—Precision, Technical Reasoning and Confluence. In each case, the person uses indicators of the single Avoid Process and the three Use First Learning Processes, thus, making the pull among the four Directional Forces distinct and powerful.

Figure 3.14 Sample Responses Strong-willed Learner

		What Makes Assignments Frustrating for You?	What Would You Do to Show What You Have Learned?
Sequence Avoid	14	Having to follow someone else's directions.	
Precision Use First	25	Not getting the correct or relevant information necessary to get the job done right.	
Technical Reasoning Use First	32	Working with people who get hung up on a concept that is obvious to me and trying to bring them to my way of thinking.	Demonstrate what I had learned in solving any problem I encounter when completing a task working alone.
Confluence Use First	25		Try something new and different.

This final sample is interesting and somewhat rare. It illustrates what a person might write if she Uses all four Patterns As Needed. Notice this individual uses no Use First and no Avoid Patterns.

Figure 3.15 Sample Responses Bridge Learner

	What Makes Assignments Frustrating for You?	What Would You Do to Show What You Have Learned?
Sequence Use As Needed 23	Nothing comes to mind. I'm pretty comfortable with following directions and finding answers. If I have a question, I'll check with someone in my group.	Listen to others' reactions and comments and then share my thoughts; you learn more when people share what they have learned.
Precision 22 Use As Needed		
Technical Reasoning 19 Use As Needed		
Confluence 22 Use as Needed		

Only 3 in 100 persons fall into this mix of Learning Processes. To verify if this Compass Rose is yours, you will want to check to see if you wrote about working and learning from others, sharing ideas, and listening. A more extensive description of a Bridge can be found under Your Compass Rose and Leadership.

The Importance of Boxing
Your Compass Rose Accurately

If you are going to Box your Compass accurately so that you truly can use it to navigate your life, then you will want to make certain that the Patterns you have identified as Use First, Use As Needed, and Avoid are accurately captured by your scores and carefully depicted by your written responses. Comparing your scores for each Pattern with what you wrote for your short answers and finding that what you wrote matches your Pattern scores means you have Boxed your Compass well!

Another means for checking your match between what you wrote and your Scale Scores is to listen to yourself talk. Certain phrases or comments clearly indicate your use of your Learning Processes. The most common comments are found in Recognizing Learning Patterns at Work. (See Appendix B.)

Ninety percent of the people who complete the LCI have results that show a variation of scores among their four Patterns. (See previous Figures 3.12-3.15.) LCI Scale Scores that show no variability would appear as Sequence 21, Precision 22, Technical Reasoning 21, and Confluence 20 or some similar combination of flat-lined scores. If you are a person who falls into the 10% that does not have variability of scores in the range of Use First, Use As Needed, and Avoid or no variability among the four Patterns, you will need to return to the LCI in Appendix A and revisit your answers. For example, did you respond to the statements using Sometimes frequently because you thought it was the safest answer? If so, you need to reconsider your responses, asking yourself, "Does my response reflect a thoughtful determination of how frequently I do something, or did I choose

Sometimes because I couldn't make up my mind?" Remember, Sometimes isn't the isle you swim to when you find yourself in the sea of indecision!

Also, if you have no Use First Patterns but you have registered a score that is a 24, you will need to revisit the questions that apply specifically to that category. One approach to resolving the dilemma of a score that sits on the cusp of Use First and Use As Needed is to see if you responded to any of the questions using an "Always" or a "Never" response. If you did not use either of the extremes of the continuum because for you, nothing is *ever* always or never, then your level of Precision is holding you back from selecting a specific answer. Add an additional point to each score that computed as 24, which is just on the brink of the Use First level. This will result in a more accurate set of Scale Scores and, therefore, a more reliable Compass Rose.

Your Compass Rose and Leadership

An important result of identifying and understanding your personal Compass Rose is that your Compass Rose of Learning also serves as a Compass Rose of leading. Your Directional Forces, which shape your approach to learning, have the same effect on your leadership. For example, if your personal Compass Rose consists of Use First Sequence and Precision, then those whom you lead can be assured that meetings will always be based on a set and orderly agenda and will be run according to it.

If your Compass Rose indicates you use Precision and Confluence at a Use First level but Avoid Sequence, then those attending your meeting need to come prepared to be led by the moment. Whatever is the hot topic or whatever is brought to the forefront at the convening of the meeting will be given equal attention to those things already on the agenda, the table, or the mind of the leader. The meeting agenda will grow by opportunity rather than by design.

Just as we learn through the influence of our personal Compass Rose on our brain-mind connection, we lead through the guiding forces of our personal Compass Rose. We need to understand and explore the implications of this in the same light as we do our Learning Processes.

One aspect of your leadership affected by your Compass Rose is the number of Patterns you Use First. If you use one or two Patterns at the Use First level, you are a *Dynamic Leader*. The point here is your Patterns do not work in isolation nor do they provide you with a single label or identity. You are *never* only one Pattern, one Directional Force. Your Compass Rose always consists of all four Patterns working as a team. Your Patterns, therefore acting in concert with each other, create a wholeness, a dynamic for success.

If your Compass Rose consists of no Use First scores (25 to 35) or Avoid scores (7 to 17), a rarity as mentioned earlier, then you lead from the middle, *Bridging* the competing factions and seeking to bring all members of the team's ideas and perspectives to the table to be heard.

I have found 3% or less of the population neither Avoid nor Use First any of the Patterns. They are comfortable using all of their Patterns, but they feel no urgency to use one over another. These individuals serve a very helpful role as Bridges. They lead from the middle, employing their Use As Needed Patterns to have a powerful impact on their team's effort. One

Bridge leader described being a Bridge in this manner: "I don't need the spotlight; I just want to contribute in my quiet way."

The Bridge Leader learns by listening to others and interacting with them. Frequently, these individuals will say things like, "I feel like a jack-of-all-trades and a master of none, but I find I can blend in, pitch in, and help make things happen as a contributing member of the group. I weigh things in the balance carefully before I act. I lead from the middle by encouraging others rather than taking charge of a situation." These leaders are team catalysts who by listening and interacting with others bring them closer to resolution while eliminating grandstanding and arguing. These individuals use phrases such as, "If I were you, I might consider," and offer quiet alternatives rather than specific demands. The Bridge is the comma that gives pause and the semicolon that connects disparate pieces.

Much more common than the Bridge Leader is the leader who uses at least three or more Patterns at the Use First level. These I term *Strong-willed Leaders*. Approximately 25% to 30% of persons holding formal leadership roles fall into this category. Whether through self-promotion or self-selection, these individuals seek out opportunities to lead rather than be led. Their Compass Rose of three or more Use First Learning Patterns positions these individuals to be their own self-contained team. Because they have flexibility in their Learning Processes, they seldom find themselves "stuck," and they prefer to control the plan, the ideas, the talks, the decisions, the processes, and the outcomes. This often makes it difficult for them to work with others. They can be critical of others who they perceive as not getting on board fast enough or not carrying their load. They lead from "out in front" rather than from the middle.

Those who are under their leadership sometimes find it difficult to follow the guidance of the Strong-willed Leader's Compass Rose, and Strong-willed Leaders often do not recognize the difficulty that their approach causes for their subordinates or their teammates. Understanding themselves as learners and being reflective about how their approach is impacting those around them is particularly important for leaders with a Strong-willed Compass Rose.

Your Compass Rose and the Voyage Ahead

In these first three chapters, you have identified your True North, framed the Directional Forces of your personal Compass Rose, explored the components that make up your brain-mind connection, and established the degree of influence your Compass Rose has on your learning and your leading.

In the next three chapters, under the heading of "Staying the Course," you will be guided in developing additional tools to help you navigate your life and your learning. Meanwhile, try your hand at boxing your personal Compass Rose. The directions for tackling this task are given next.

Boxing the Compass

- Boxing your personal Compass Rose is essential to understanding how to navigate your life because all of life's ventures rely on your ability to use your Learning Processes well.

- Boxing your Compass Rose allows you to understand your leadership behaviors and others' response to them.
- Boxing your Compass Rose is a very personal and powerful experience.

Taking Stock

- Think about two assignments that you have been given recently, one that was hard for you and one that was easy. Take the Directional Forces that make up your Compass Rose (your Learning Patterns) and use them to analyze why you found one task difficult and the other one easy.
- Develop a written profile of your Compass Rose using the following as a model. Note that you will fill in your actual LCI Scale Scores. Then below each of the Directional Forces (Sequence, Precision, Technical Reasoning, and Confluence), you will write a brief description of how you use that Learning Process in your personal and professional life. Read through Figure 3.12 to see how to put the Learning Process descriptions you read about in this chapter into your own words.

Figure 3.16 Description of My Personal Compass
Rose (Sample)

A Description of My Personal
Compass Rose

SAMPLE

	Avoid	Use as Needed	Use First
Sequence	09		
Precision		21	
Technical		19	
Confluent			33

EXPLANATION

Sequence:

I am a person who avoids directions. They just don't make sense to me. The most I can
handle is a three-step process. After that I prefer to figure it out on my own.

Precision:

I use precision as needed. While I read a lot, I don't read non-fiction, factual books.
I do research and dig into information when I am interested in a topic. I don't seek
information just to know facts. I am not a walking almanac of minutia.

Technical:

I use my technical as needed similar to my precision. The part of technical that I relate
to best is being able to work by myself. I am a loner not a joiner. I want just the right
tool to get a job done, and I love gadgets, but I don't care how things work nor am
I interested in fixing things.

Confluence:

I use my confluence as the leader of my personal learning team. I never met an idea
I didn't like. If I do something once, the second time it becomes overworked and the
third time boring. I like the excitement of pushing the envelope.

Figure 3.17 Description of My Personal Compass Rose (Blank)

A Description of My Personal Compass Rose

SAMPLE

	Avoid	Use as Needed	Use First
Sequence			
Precision			
Technical			
Confluent			

EXPLANATION

Sequence:

Precision:

Technical:

Confluence:

PART II

FINDING YOUR WAY:
STAYING THE COURSE

4. All Hands on Deck

"The individual can fail,
but the team cannot."

—Eugene Kranz (1977)
Mission Director, Apollo 13

The Focus

- Teaming our Directional Forces
- Understanding the internal talk of our learning

Our brain-mind connection is the captain of our vessel, our navigator. The "crew" that carries out the captain's orders consists of the Directional Forces in our minds, our Compass Rose. This chapter concerns how to use your full crew to navigate your life, your career, and your relationships.

Not only do you need "all hands on deck" to succeed in your life but also you need to build this motley crew of processes into a fine-tuned team prepared to respond to any idea, task, or challenging situation that confronts it. The strategic use of your crew of processes is called *metacognition*. In fact, for the purpose of this text, we might label them "Team Metacognition." Understanding our metacognition is central to using our navigational Compass Rose with success.

Straightforward, metacognition is the internal talk that goes on in your mind among your team of Learning Processes. This is your crew of Learning Processes "chatter," as one calls to another—expressing its feelings, its concerns, or the action it wants to engage in. Imagine one crew member sitting high above in the crow's nest of the ship calling to a crew member on a yardarm while yet another is manning the helm or swabbing the deck. All are important members of the crew; all are taking in the world around them and processing it. But each has a different perspective.

The communication that goes on among your Learning Processes forms your metacognition. Rather than ignore the chatter or discount it as a distraction, actively listen to how your Patterns talk to one another in your mind, pulling and tugging you in different directions. Then take charge and talk back to them, employing strategies that help you use one or more of your Patterns successfully to complete the assignment or task you have been given.

If you learn to acknowledge and listen to your internal metacognitive chatter, you can begin to take charge of your response to it. The empowering, central point of *Finding Your Way* is that when you navigate your daily life aware of your Compass Rose and your metacognitive chatter—you can set a course and stay that course to a successful completion.

The Story

This chapter's story focuses on the Apollo 13 space voyage. Decades after the words, "Houston, we have a problem," were uttered, they continue to alert anyone who hears them that the project being ventured is in serious trouble! Just as these words are used to alert us to a problem, the response attributed to Apollo 13's mission control director is repeated with equal frequency: "Failure is not an option!"

Most of us know the story of Apollo 13. Some of us lived every moment of it as we tracked the unfolding of what appeared to be a space voyage disaster in the making. Others know the story based on its retelling in the movie *Apollo 13*.

Those who saw the film remember one of its most dramatic moments. Facing the nearly impossible task of bringing the astronauts home despite the spacecraft's loss of oxygen and power, the support teams at the Houston Space Center were challenged to create equipment that would allow the astronauts to power up the craft using only the materials and equipment available to them on the spacecraft itself. In the film, various teams sorted through piles of disparate items dumped on a table in front of them, seeking to convert trash into functioning systems.

Although offering a less cinematic depiction of the situation, Michael Useem (1998), in his book, *The Leadership Moment*, related the urgency of the situation as he described how Eugene Kranz, the 36-year-old mission director, communicated and interacted with his various mission control teams. Constantly aware that this was a life-and-death situation, Kranz drew on the knowledge and expertise of his team members, listening intently to their minute-by-minute updates, calculating the options, and weighing in the balance how to avoid failure and to achieve a lifesaving outcome. Useem quoted Kranz as describing his job as "basically to orchestrate all the players" (p. 87) and to bring "the team together" (p. 80).

Key insights can be gained from deconstructing the Apollo 13 story. These insights focus not only on the leadership of Kranz during the crisis, but even more on the preparation of teams led by Kranz prior to the launch and the ensuing crisis. Much of Kranz's approach to teams is applicable to our internal metacognitive team of Learning Processes. In the learning that follows, note the importance of listening to the various Processes and then learn when and how to use them with intention to solve any problem or dilemma that confronts you. This is the first step in taking control of how you learn and in making it work for you. Once that begins you can successfully navigate your interactions with others, whether at home or at work.

The Learning

What we learn from Apollo 13 is that to function under duress, we need to have formed our teams well. We need to know the team members—including their assets, their expertise, how well they work with others, and their abilities as communicators. Then we need to do the following:

- Listen to them
- Consult with them
- Rehearse them thoroughly under a variety of circumstances
- Make them interchangeable
- Use their insights strategically to inform our leadership decisions

The Apollo 13 story lends itself well to understanding how to use our internal team of Learning Processes to navigate our lives. Just as mission control did, you and I need to know what the makeup of our team of Patterns is, understand how the pieces communicate with one another, and recognize the expertise each brings to a given situation. When we listen to the internal talk of our Learning Processes, our metacognitive team, we are able to harness the pull of our True North to the directional guidance of our Compass Rose to give us our bearing and to set us on a course that is most likely to succeed.

I cannot overemphasize this point. Taking time to listen to your team of Learning Processes is vital. Listening is more than hearing. Listening is the conscious processing of what you hear.

True listening yields attentiveness and allows you to weigh in the balance the various perspectives you are hearing so you can then act.

Missing the Message of Team Metacognition

I think that often we miss the voice of our metacognition because we are overstimulated with ringtone cells, blasting video games, or deafening music. We spend a great deal of time trying *not* to hear—*not* to listen to our minds at work. To ignore that conversation is to say to the Compass Rose of our learning, "I am not interested in your directional voice. I am not willing to listen to you advocate within me as my best source of coaching and development. I am going to drown you out with busyness. I am going to stifle your insights. I'm going to ignore the clear directional guides you are seeking to provide me. Besides, I can't make out all that you are saying. Your static is distracting, even irritating. Get your act together before you try to communicate your message to me. Give me a single straightforward message, not a series of whispers and shouts all tangled together."

To an extent, we *do* have a right to ask our metacognition to clarify its message. It would be so simple if we heard one clear, direct instruction. But we don't because our mind, our Compass Rose of Directional Forces, does not speak with simple one-liners. Our metacognition doesn't speak with one voice. Our metacognition is comprised of a quartet of tones. It challenges us to hear the harmony and disharmony; it alerts us to potential discords within us or among the people with whom we are working. It forces us to listen and then make defining decisions.

For example, if my Sequence is crying out that it is over-whelmed, I need to hear that. If my Confluence is seeking attention by pumping one idea on top of another, I need to acknowledge it while taking action to turn down its volume. I need to salve my hurting Sequence and find a means to strengthen it for the task ahead.

Metacognition is our internal talk—the voice of our Patterns telling, arguing, and negotiating how to proceed, how to achieve, and how to reach our destination. Hearing the metacognition in us takes practice, patience, and skill. By using your crew of Learning Processes, you will be using the most powerful personal navigational tool you possess. You will have at your ready your thinking skills, your power to act, and your True North embedded in each aspect of your decisions. There is no more powerful combination of human resources for directing your life journey.

Listening to Your Metacognition and Attending to Its Midcourse Corrections

Metacognition consists of the voices of your Patterns as they seek to resolve how to plot a course for success. Metacognition, however, is not passive. It is active. It is constantly checking to see if you are on or off course. It does so through a series of phases, a continuum of activities that help you check your progress and position you to stay the course. I have ascribed action verbs to represent each phase of metacognition: *Mull, Connect, Rehearse, Express, Assess, Reflect,* and *Revisit.* (See Figure 4.2.) Throughout the phases, the discussion among your Patterns continues. Even as you are setting your course, you are already employing your metacognitive actions.

Most often, we plot our course by using our metacognitive action phases in order. However, because the degrees to which we use our Directional Forces differ, the manner in which we use our metacognition also differs. We sometimes begin at the beginning and Mull, but other times we jump into a situation in the middle and just begin to Express. As you read through the explanation of each term, you will be able to identify specific instances when you have used all or some of the phases in or out of order.

Figure 4.2 Metacognitive Drill

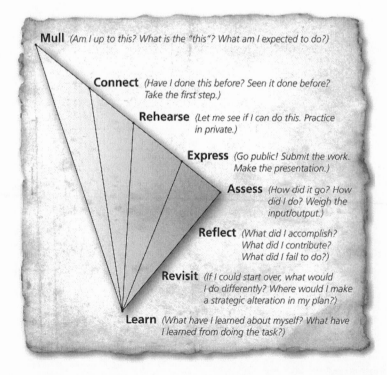

Mull

Virtually all tasks begin with some form of Mulling. "What am I being asked to do? Have I ever done this before? What were the results? Do I want to repeat those results or avoid them?" You stay firmly anchored until you have a sense of where you are going and how you are going to prepare for the venture. Mulling is healthy; stewing isn't. If the voices of your Patterns are crying out for clearer directions or a greater sense of purpose, then listen and ask for what you need.

Connect

If you have Mulled successfully, then almost seamlessly you begin to make connections to the requirements of the task. You collect your thoughts, review your options, and prepare for the venture. You gather your resources, talk with others who may have taken on a similar task, compare your task to theirs, note the differences and similarities, and begin to accumulate the resources you will need to support and sustain your plan. The Connect aspect of your metacognition has your Pattern of Sequence working diligently and your Pattern of Precision equally hustling, scouring for pertinent data. Your Technical Reasoning is in survival mode while your Confluence is holding back because it doesn't enjoy basing the future on the past. It would much rather skip the Connecting phase and get to the make-or-break action. If you are wise, you will ignore the folly offered by your Confluence and allow your other Patterns to guide you in connecting fully and completely with the task at hand.

Rehearse-Express

The next metacognitive checkpoint for course corrections involves two joint phases, Rehearse-Express. The Rehearse phase allows your Patterns to go through a trial run in your head to make certain that the performance of the task, the completion of the project, and/or the public presentation of the outcomes will meet the standards originally set. Rehearsal prepares for expression by allowing any mistakes to be assessed and corrected. This is where your Sequence will shine to whatever degree it comprises your Compass Rose and your Precision will work to take corrective action.

Expression, actually doing what was practiced, is the "going public" side of Rehearsal. Expression is no longer the test run but the real thing. Although your Processes of Sequence and Precision particularly enjoyed Rehearsal, they are not at ease during the Express phase.

During Express, you will hear a greater tension in the internal talk of Sequence and Precision. They want their Rehearsal to pay off with perfection. Rehearse-perform is their mantra. Technical Reasoning, on the other hand, is fired up because the long awaited time for action has finally arrived! Meanwhile, Confluence, which was yawning during Rehearsal and questioning how many times you have to go over the same thing, is ready to Express! In fact, Use First Confluence would much prefer to do this live, with no Rehearsal, no safety nets, and no lifeboats. During this metacognitive phase, Confluence is not bounded by the compunction of Precision for perfection. If you are aware of how the voice of Confluence can, like the Sirens of Greek mythology, seek to pull you off course, then you will be able to quiet their influence and hold steady to the course of Rehearse-Express. In fact, you will prepare fully and completely for any and all exigencies.

The final phases of metacognition join with the initial phases to create a reflective practice feedback loop. When you enter into these phases, you are in both a vulnerable and an enviable position. If you sail through this set of phases unscathed, then you have, indeed, used your Compass Rose well, allowing you to not only stay your course but also come safe home. On the other hand, missteps and challenges along the way will help you learn how to empower your course correction capacity for the next learning voyage.

Assess

Metacognition, when faithfully followed, will always include a time to Assess. Unlike external assessment or "testing," the Assess of metacognition means confronting questions such as, "What have I really achieved?" and "To what degree have I achieved it?" Jim Collins (2001), in his book *Good to Great*, refers to this as facing your current reality. What is the outcome of your effort? What are the quantitative and qualitative results? This is when you need to let the data lead you to confront what was achieved as a result of your efforts. The metacognitive phase that follows focuses on the words of the prior question, "as a result of your efforts," because reflection requires a long hard look at yourself.

Reflect

When you Reflect you ask, "Where does the buck stop? Who is responsible for this success? This failure? This mess?" This is the piece of professional and personal growth you may have been missing. You see, anyone can use the phrase, "mistakes have been made," to attribute failure and blame anonymously. But only mindful individuals with a clear sense of their personal True North and Compass Rose of Directional Forces can face their self-imposed mirror and say precisely, "I screwed up, and I am prepared to take the heat for it." Interestingly, this is where Technical Reasoning can assume too much responsibility, believing that it is the sole factor that determines the success or failure of an operation. It is important to examine the contribution of each Directional Force to one's success or failure—to consider the totality of the effect of Team Metacognition on the final outcome.

Using your metacognition well equips you to stay the course of your metacognitive phases until you reach a powerful self-awareness. It is only if you stay the course and reflect that you become willing to ask, "Confronted with the same situation, what would I personally do differently? How would I recalculate, rethink, replot, and reequip?" With a new maturity and sense of self, you can do this without ever pointing to anyone but yourself and reflecting on the outcome.

You are now ready to use reflective practice to ask which of the espoused values of your True North you abandoned along the way. Ask yourself the following: What did I allow myself to do? What did I allow myself to fail to do? Where did my

Compass Rose, my Directional Learning Processes, steer me off course?

This is the autopsy of failure. Without it, you are doomed to continue to achieve less than you could. You cannot continue to repeat your actions, believing that they will yield a different outcome. Interestingly, this is where our Confluence can lead us because Confluence understands failure. Confluence learns from failure in a manner that it does not from the Connecting and Rehearsal phases that it frequently chooses to ignore or skip completely. Confluence, when confronted with failure, immediately and willingly seeks to understand what, in retrospect, it could not grasp in the planning phase. Listen to the Confluence of your Compass Rose, and let it lead you fearlessly through this vital phase.

Reflection requires us to face ourselves, specifically the totality of who we are and how we have used our Compass Rose, our metacognitive talk, and our self-correcting opportunities or how we have failed to do so. This is the heart of *Finding Your Way*.

Revisit

The good news found in reflective practice is that it does not conclude with assigning blame and shame or with rewarding success. Instead, Reflective practice invites you to Revisit your metacognitive phases, noting both those that enriched and those that frustrated your venture. Revisiting metacognitive decisions serves to reinforce the specific strategies that led to success and reconsider those that led to failure. Revisiting grows metacognitive capacity and personal insight.

You may have noted that at each stage of the metacognitive continuum (Mull, Connect, Rehearse-Express, Assess, Reflect, and Revisit)—the conversation among your Directional Forces changes—actually develops and evolves. The more frequently we tune in to it, the more clearly we can identify the direction we are being given. Our team of Learning Processes and their metacognitive talk make it possible for us to stay the course.

Putting the Learning into Practice

Metacognition is also crucial on the high seas of the work world. The opening pages of this book related several work scenarios. Among them was one where you were tasked to write a summary of a meeting that had just occurred. I want to revisit that task, applying what we have discussed so far about our Compass Rose of Learning Processes. Here, for the reader's convenience, is a recounting of the task:

Write a brief summary of your most recent team meeting.

Clearly, this is not much of a challenge for a professional or any competent adult. In fact, the words "brief summary" indicate that this is something you can complete quickly. Yet you find yourself procrastinating—doing anything else to avoid the dreaded writing task. Then again, maybe it isn't the task but how it is framed that's causing you frustration. You find that you actually resent the word "brief." You think to yourself, "That was a very important session we just completed. Brief won't do the job. The folks not present will really be left out of the loop if they don't receive a blow-by-blow of what transpired. How am I going to be brief *and* thorough?"

Or maybe you sat down, cranked out the summary, and e-mailed it within 30 minutes of receiving the assignment— only to read later that afternoon that you supervisor has rethought the brief summary assignment and now wants a more thorough accounting, including graphs and charts. Your frustration over the change in directions requires you to pop an antacid or Prozac.

Having completed the first three chapters of this text, you are now well aware that the descriptions of the individual responses to the writing task are based on each individual's Compass Rose. In addition, you also understand that the writing task isn't just a simple remembering and writing exercise. Instead, the task requires a very sophisticated use of an individual's brain-mind connection. Writing actually requires you to express, articulate, and communicate thoughts, feelings, experiences, and ideas in symbolic representation by consistently using lines scratched on paper. These scratches or preset lines must have the same meaning each time they are viewed by the human eye and translated by the brain's neuroreceptors. Their meaning and intent must stay consistent even as they pass through the various Learning Processes of Sequence, Precision, Technical Reasoning, and Confluence and are interpreted and stored by the working memory. Those squiggles on paper must carry to another person the same tone, message, and perspective that the writer intended. That is a lot to ask of them!

Suddenly, writing becomes a set of brain-mind challenges. So although the task is to write a brief summary, the task is not a simple one! And on top of that, you now know that the message needs to pass over the ocean of the recipient's brain-mind connection and then be guided by that person's Compass Rose to come into the intended port with a bill of lading labeled "full comprehension."

It is the metacognition of our Compass Rose that navigates the issues confronting us when we are working to complete a task. Take, for instance, the writing task reviewed earlier. Let's say that your Compass Rose is one that Avoids Precision and uses Technical Reasoning at the Use First level (Sequence 22, Precision 15, Technical Reasoning 28, and Confluence 23). A writing task is typically the last thing you will want to complete. The procrastination is simply one way of putting off your struggle with words. Those who Avoid Precision don't like dealing with words, and will find it difficult to discern what are the most important facts or information to convey because they all seem equally important and equally overwhelming; those who are Use First Technical Reasoning relish working in other symbol forms and declare that words aren't their tool of choice. Combined, these two Processes can make the task seem monumental. Here is where your awareness of your Metacognitive Process can come in very handy.

Your Compass Rose as a Team Effort

First, instead of waiting to be rescued, you can pull yourself out of the doldrums and make your way by looking to the other Directional Forces that make up your Compass Rose. Yes, it's true that you have two that seem to be working against you (Precision 15 and Technical Reasoning 28) when it comes to completing the task, but you also have two other Patterns that will help you listen (Sequence 22 and Confluence 23). So far, their voices have been muffled by the whining of your Avoid Precision and Use First Technical Reasoning. However, to ignore these other members of your team is to flounder when you could be sailing through the task.

Here is how your other two Processes can contribute. Because your Confluence is at the high side of Use As Needed, let's look at it first as a possible place to start. Interestingly, your Confluence offers an idea for where to begin. It suggests to your team of Directional Forces that you can use your Use As Needed Sequence to organize three specific points to record as the most significant pieces of information to come out of the meeting. Your Sequence also suggests that you Revisit the agenda for the meeting to identify the key points you need to recount, thereby rescuing your Avoid Precision from having to determine what to include in the report and what to leave out.

Because of this efficient way of approaching the task, your Technical Reasoning suddenly seems energized. It can see the purpose in what you are doing.

Meanwhile, your Precision begins to come alive, feeling less and less overwhelmed. This is teamwork in action! Is this team strategy a lot to consider? Yes. Important to consider? Vital! Possible to understand? Absolutely! Can it make all the difference in whether you stay the course and complete the task in a professional manner? Yes, indeed.

There is no doubt that when you understand your Compass Rose and the internal talk of your Patterns as they work through the various metacognitive phases, you are well equipped, as Peter Senge (1999) described, "to consistently enhance your capacity to produce results that are truly important to you" (p. 45).

Boxing the Compass

- What metacognition teaches us is that our Directional Forces (Learning Processes) each have a voice that is available to us and that can help us navigate any task, assignment, or project.
- Meanwhile, our metacognition guides our course and plots any midcourse corrections should the need arise.

Taking Stock

- Think about the last time you had a really bad feeling when you were given a work task. Using your new understanding of your Learning Processes and the internal talk that each uses, can you identify what conflict among your Processes might have been causing you to have that reaction?
- Think about a time when you were experiencing a lot of metacognitive internal talk. Was it positive and empowering or was it negative? Develop a graphic representation that would explain the internal talk, noting the various metacognitive phases you were in as you worked your way through the situation. Label aspects of the visual with the metacognitive terms that follow: Mull, Connect, Rehearse, Express, Assess, Reflect, Revisit, and Learn.

- What kind of a team player are you? Using your Compass Rose, make a list of what Directional Forces you specifically bring to a team and what you need from the team.

Insights

5. Adrift in Uncharted Waters

"Success in today's global environment will
depend upon how well people can learn
and apply new ideas and skills effectively."
—Noreen Campbell, 2000
Operations Manager(ret.)

The Focus

- Understanding the logistics of personal learning
- Understanding the strategic use of one's Compass Rose

I chose the title of this chapter, "Adrift in Uncharted Waters," with care. I meant to juxtapose it against the focus of this segment of the book, staying the course, because I think being able to accomplish the latter, within the context of the former, is a real sign of personal and professional growth. To be able to stay the course even when you find yourself dealing with the not previously experienced and the unknown is a vital skill and not one that you and I can develop without self-awareness of our True North and Compass Rose.

Working in uncharted waters represents one area of our lives that is very common in our work and personal interactions. It confronts us daily. It can throw us off and determine whether we are going to have a good day or a not-so-good day. Why? Because life, for the most part, runs well as long as it runs consistently. Throw in a disruption to your schedule, a change in your route to work, or an emergency of any degree, and you find yourself saying, "Well, now what? What am I supposed to do? How am I going to handle that?"

Uncharted waters can also include a change in plans, a new task, a new team assignment, a new employee, or the arrival of a different stage of development for your marriage and family. Uncharted waters can be anything that you haven't planned for and are now confronted with. Uncharted waters are what most frequently appear to make our lives, our work, and our relationships fall apart. Uncharted waters are the unexpected, unanticipated, or the new with no directions attached. I love the title of a parenting book that really nails this issue: *Got the Baby Where's the Manual?* (Baum, 2007). Uncharted waters for certain!

In the Introduction to this book I asked, "Have you ever been lost?" Then I explained, *"Finding Your Way* is structured to guide you on a very interactive and personal journey. You will discover how to use your mind with intention—that is with consciousness of what you are doing and why you are doing it—to absorb information and develop skills and judgment through self-directed assessment and personal reflection. *Finding Your Way* addresses various aspects of the reader's personal learning journey and guides the reader to use the directional tools appropriately in his or her life."

This chapter provides direction for you even under the most extreme circumstances. For the past four chapters, you have been preparing to face the challenge of uncharted waters. Now, finally, you have an opportunity to take your more complete self-awareness, provided by the development of your personal Compass Rose and your understanding of the interaction of the Learning Patterns it represents, to discover how to position yourself logistically and strategically to take on the new, the unknown, and the uncharted.

Where do you begin to develop this skill? You begin by reviewing the composition of your Compass Rose and comparing it to the requirements of the situation or the task at hand. That is, you identify the logistics or the amount of Directional Forces required to complete the task, and then you strategize how to position your Directional Forces to accomplish the task before you. When you have completed that phase, you implement, revisit the outcome, make the midcourse corrections, and keep moving toward your goal, your destination.

A Test of Navigational Skills

Three medical lab technicians in training, who use Sequence (clear directions, specific examples) and Precision (specific details, exact information) at a Use First level and Avoid Confluence (risk taking), are having difficulty solving problems similar but not identical to ones they have read about in their texts and experienced during their clinicals. One whispers to her colleagues, "I don't know what to do here." All three sit combing their minds trying to recall, "Where have I seen this problem before?"

The truth of the matter is, the problem facing them requires them to connect their prior experience to a problem similar to the one currently in front of them. They can't find the model to duplicate because of the unique nature of the one facing them. They have the skills required to solve the problem, but they can't call up the confidence to direct themselves because they have become stuck in the Connecting phase of their metacognition and the Sequence and Precision of their Compass Roses.

For these individuals, who are high in their use of Sequence and Precision, Connecting the problem in front of them means recalling a problem from their practice labs that looks *exactly* like the current one. Their Use First Sequence and Precision, coupled with their Avoidance of Confluence, keeps them from feeling comfortable moving away from the need to have something identical to a lesser exactness of something similar. When individuals with this Compass Rose of Directional Forces don't see that they can logically carry over insights from one type of problem to another, they flounder in what they perceive as uncharted waters.

The Story

Supervisors Tasked to Eliminate Errors

The persons in this story are individuals who have worked as plant operators on a production line for some 25 years. Now, because of changes in the plant, many will be moving from the plant floor to the quality-control center. They will be required to record data accurately and blend and mix chemicals accurately. In addition, each day at the end of the shift, they must hand off their phase of production to the next shift while in the midst of completing highly sensitive phases of chemical processing. Because of the plant schedule, this is not a face-to-face handoff. Instead, the hand off of information must occur through archived data and logged procedures.

The persons doing the training of the operators are, for the most part, college-educated chemists and engineers. Those receiving the training from them are primarily high school graduates who have not taken part in formal education for more than 20 years.

The average scores of the Learning Processes of those providing the instruction and those receiving the instruction are the following:

	Sequence	Precision	Technical Reasoning	Confluence
Management (Trainers)	22	28	27	24
Operators (Trainees)	27	21	22	20

You need only compare the Learning Processes of the two groups to recognize that the operators and trainers were going to be navigating in uncharted waters when they began their training and instruction. And because, initially, the two groups knew nothing about their learning selves and their Compass Roses, they did not understand the logistics of what would be needed to communicate and develop skills through either their verbal directions or their live demonstrations.

The operators complained because the supervisor/trainers "talked, talked, and talked" (Precision) but never put their information into clear steps (Sequence) that the operators could then follow. Instead, the supervisor/trainers explained in endless words (Precision) *why* something should be done but not methodically *how* it should be completed (Sequence). A breakthrough finally occurred when the directions printed in paragraphs and attached to the various pieces of plant equipment were recast as numbered steps. The response of the operators was amazing. Instead of "words, words, words," they saw "Step 1, Step 2, Step 3." With their need for Sequence met, they responded with a new degree of consistent operational performance. Problem solved!

Once success was achieved with the operational directions, the same awareness of Learning Processes was carried into the reorganizing of shift logs and the procedures for the handing off of information from one shift to the next. The reorganization of the information from paragraphs to numbered lists, and from written narratives to shift log pages with directional guides, made all the difference. The logistical and the strategic changes allowed the operators and management trainers to fuse the use of their Directional Forces into a seamless success.

Over the course of a two-year period, plant management and supervisors worked on developing monitoring processes and follow-up procedures openly requested by the operators (Sequence 27) but not done consistently by the supervisors (Sequence 22, Confluence 24).

Throughout that period, plant supervisors engaged the operators in developing strategies for helping the operators observe subtle changes in products as a part of quality control. This required intensifying the operators' use of Precision (22) when working on quality issues. At one point, the training officer developed stations that featured the different types of subtle changes the trainers wanted the operators to recognize. This allowed the operators to Rehearse-Express and practice the art of observing with greater Precision.

Plant supervisors also recognized the need to initiate audit procedures and shift procedures and to rely on the use of the Sequential strength of the operators to develop solutions to problems involving sealing and shipping the plant's product. At one point, a group of operators strategically using their Learning Processes met and developed not only a means for pinpointing what shift and which personnel were not completing a procedure correctly, but also brought forward information and ideas to rectify the situation.

By informing both operators and management of their Compass Roses of Directional Learning Processes, both operators and supervisor/trainers worked together to Decode the tasks that confronted and confounded them. They then moved to rectify the situation by building appropriate performance strategies that helped guide their on-the-job behaviors, communication, and productivity.

The use of these logistical and strategic tools in uncharted waters helped contribute to a reversal in fortune for the plant. It went from being designated "to be closed" to being designated "continue operations" as a growth business. All the while, the operators and management attentively kept a chart of their Learning Processes in the training room. They began each team training session with a review of who brought what to the team in Learning Processes and who needed what from the team to succeed in the team effort. The teams also remained alert to what Learning Process clashes could potentially cause conflict among the team's members and what the team needed to promote to achieve a high level of cooperation. At one meeting, the agenda included these remarks:

- Be aware of the balance or lack of balance among the Learning Processes of your team members and be prepared to address that openly (a strategic awareness).
- Work to figure out how you are going to overcome that imbalance (a logistic awareness).

The Thought and Action Chart presented next (See Figure 5.2.) attests to the preparation that went into readying both operators and supervisor/trainers to enter the uncharted waters of turning around a plant's future.

Figure 5.2 Decoded Procedures for Plant Operators

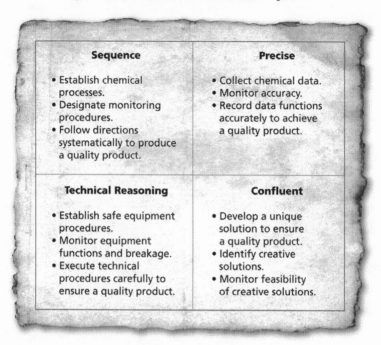

Sequence	Precise
• Establish chemical processes. • Designate monitoring procedures. • Follow directions systematically to produce a quality product.	• Collect chemical data. • Monitor accuracy. • Record data functions accurately to achieve a quality product.
Technical Reasoning	**Confluent**
• Establish safe equipment procedures. • Monitor equipment functions and breakage. • Execute technical procedures carefully to ensure a quality product.	• Develop a unique solution to ensure a quality product. • Identify creative solutions. • Monitor feasibility of creative solutions.

The Learning

There are specific navigational tools that can help you address a problem, a task, or a situation. These tools involve the following:

- The logistical tool of Decoding (analyzing the situation and determining the logistics) the resources needed to employ
- The strategic tool of FITing (Forging, Intensifying, and Tethering) the Directional Forces of your Compass Rose to "resource" the situation in an efficient, effective, and successful manner

The Logistical Tool of Decoding

The goal of Decoding is twofold: (1) to identify and clarify the intent of the directions (i.e., what exactly is this person's vision for the outcome of the assignment as seen through the direction-giver's set of Learning Processes) and (2) to identify the degree to which you are going to be required to use your Learning Processes to accomplish the task as per this individual's envisioned outcome.

When we understand our personal Directional Forces, we can direct them to take specific action. Using the knowledge of our Learning Processes and the cue words that are used to indicate what Processes are required to complete the task, we can Decode assignments, objectives, or the task at hand. We can look for key words in a set of directions and engage our specific Compass Rose of Processes (Sequence, Precision, Technical Reasoning, or Confluence) to accomplish the task.

Decoding tasks accurately is the first step to navigating uncharted waters. Using the example that follows, examine how Decoding works:

- First, read the guidelines or directions for the task.
- Next, circle the key words that are intended to direct your action.
- Then, label each according to the Learning Process it is directing you to use. To do this you will want to refer to the Directional Force Word Wall (See Figure 5.3.), a chart of words categorized by the Directional Force each requires.
- Finally, analyze the amount of time you need to invest in using each of your Processes, each portion of your Compass Rose of Learning, to complete the task successfully.

Figure 5.3 Directional Forces Word Wall

Sequence		Precision	
alphabetize	order	calibrate	label
arrange	organize	detail	measure
classify	pros and cons	describe	name
compare and contrast	put in a series	document	record (facts)
develop	put in order	examine	observe
distribute	sequence	explain	perform accurately
group	show an array	identify	specify
list	show an example		

Technical Reasoning		Confluence	
assemble	figure out	act carefree	imagine
build	fix	brainstorm	improvise
construct	implement	chance	innovate
demonstrate	just do it	concoct	invent
engineer	operate concretely	create	originate
erect	problem solve	dream-up	risk
experience	represent graphically	make-up	take a chance

As you read and complete the three sample decoding tasks, observe how the Directional Forces Word Wall guides you in Decoding or accurately labeling the key words contained in each task's directions.

Task I

- Write in bulleted form a brief description of the new security operation.

Begin the Decoding process by circling the key words of the task. Next, locate each circled word on the Directional Forces Word Wall, identifying the category in which the words are located. Finally, label each word using S = Sequence required, P = Precision required, T = Technical problem solving required, C = Confluence required.

When you are finished, your Decoded task should look like the sentence found in Figure 5.4.

Figure 5.4 Decoded Task I

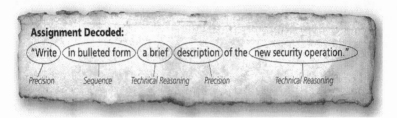

At this point, you may be thinking that this is a great deal of work just to understand what appears to be a straightforward task. And that may be true if your Learning Processes match the requirements of the task to a *T*. But let's consider what could occur if your Directional Forces, your Learning Processes, were the following: Sequence 28, Precision 17, Technical Reasoning 26, and Confluence 21. With that Compass Rose of Learning Processes and *without* Decoding the task in its entirety, you may allow your Compass Rose to shut down as soon as your Avoid Precision (17) reads the word "write." Why? Because with an Avoid in Precision writing is something you just don't want to do!

If you allow your Avoidance of Precision to keep you from reading the rest of the task description, you will fail when, in fact, you could succeed by using your Technical Reasoning and Sequential Patterns to overcome the frustration of Avoiding Precision!

If you had Decoded the task first, you would be able to make strategic moves to keep your Directional Forces focused on how to complete the task successfully.

The second example that follows (See Figure 5.5.) reinforces the importance of Decoding a task before beginning it.

Task II

- Make specific recommendations to solve the current cash flow problem.

Once again, by circling key words and labeling them, you discover that the task involves more than composing a list of general recommendations or off-the-cuff ideas on paper. This task requires the use of Precision to determine carefully crafted recommendations that are the result of examining the organization's cash flow (Sequence) and considering various approaches to solve (Technical Reasoning) the current specific problems.

Figure 5.5 Decoding Task II

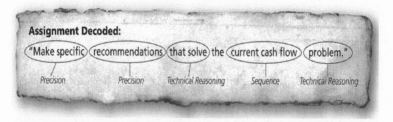

Again, take time to examine how the task was Decoded and how the Decoding reveals the degree to which you are required to use each of your Directional Forces to succeed.

Now it's time for you to Decode a real-world task using *your* actual Compass Rose of Learning Processes. Begin by recording your Directional Learning Processes on the lines provided:

Sequence __Precision __Technical__Confluence__Reasoning

Now, try your hand at Decoding the task described.

Task III

- Identify and list the pros and cons of implementing radio frequency identification (RFID) to garden supplies, perishable items, and electronics. Compare the recovered costs resulting from loss stoppage and potential reassigned crew time against start-up expenses of implementing the system.

First, Decode and label the key words of the task. Next, analyze the degree to which you will be required to use your Learning Processes to complete each aspect of the work assignment. Then ask, logistically, what type and amount of Directional Forces are going to be required to complete this task? Can you identify the point when you will need to be using one portion of your Compass Rose more than another? Overall, do you have the resources to carry out the task? The knowledge? The depth of Directional Forces to complete it? If not, can you draw on another member of your team to provide the missing portion? To see the correctly Decoded task, turn to Figure 5.6 and examine how the key terms of the task were identified and labeled. How does your Decoding of the task compare?

Figure 5.6 Decoding Task III

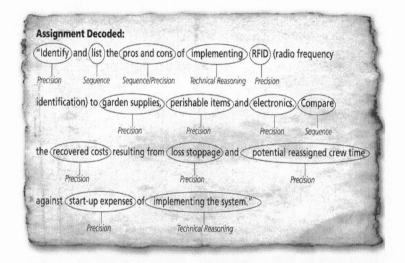

This task clearly requires a significant amount of Precision (a total of 10 terms requiring Precision), a strategic use of Sequence to list and compare (two references), a great deal of Technical Reasoning to implement the new process effectively (two references), and no Confluence. This task does not invite a flight of mind or playing with the facts!

Knowing the mental resources required to complete a specific task helps assuage the feeling that you are in uncharted waters. Using the logistical tool of Decoding allows you to feel informed and prepared for the task at hand. Using the strategic tool of FITing completes the "gearing up" that is necessary to be prepared to take on uncharted waters.

The Strategic Tool of FITing

The purpose of the second tool is to match the action of your Compass Rose to the task at hand by FITing your Directional

Forces to the required action. (FIT is an acronym for Forge, Intensify, and Tether). In other words, learning to FIT your Learning Processes to the situation means that you can specifically match your Compass Rose of Learning Processes to the task at hand by providing sufficient directional energy to accomplishing the task you are facing.

Forge

The term Forge is intended to be applied to those Directional Forces that fall between 7 and 17 on the Learning Connections Inventory (LCI) Scoring Scale. The purpose of Forging a Directional Force is to increase the use and performance of it. Forging requires you to zero in with a laser focus on a Process you would just as soon forget about. However, when Forging, you seek to use different aspects of the Avoid Process to make proper and appropriate use of it as per the directions provided for the task. Impossible? No. Does it require your attention and intention? Absolutely! It also requires an increased use of mental energy.

Regardless of which Process you need to Forge or how many Processes you Avoid, the amount of mental energy you need to alter a Directional Force's natural level of performance is directly related to the degree to which you Avoid it.

For example, my LCI score in Sequence is 9. I Avoid Sequence to a great degree. To Forge this, I need to employ an extraordinary amount of energy to expand it, increase its volume, and move it to a greater level of proficiency. I also need to recognize that this state of Forging has its limits. I can only Forge for an additional five points (9 + 5 = 14), which is still in the Avoid category (but better!), and I can only sustain that intensity of energy for a brief period—a few minutes, several hours, possibly two or three days. Then the Directional Force will return to its natural level of use.

Therefore, keep in mind that when you are required to Forge an Avoid Process for a significant period, you will not have your same energy level to devote to coping with your other Learning Processes.

Take for instance the following task, common to most work situations:

- Submit an itemized list of expenditures from oldest to most recent. Then, using a two-column format, compare last year's expenditures to this year's.

When I read words that call for the use of Sequence (alphabetize, categorize, compare, list, organize), I immediately sense that I am being asked to enter uncharted waters. I know that if I am to succeed, I need to explore carefully what I am being asked to do, and then identify what personal strategies I will engage in to navigate my way through the task. (See a list of strategies relating to each Directional Force of your Compass Rose at the conclusion of this chapter, Figure 5.9.)

As I reread the requirements, my metacognitive talk rises to a survival level, requiring all hands on deck. Because I know that I Avoid Sequence, I seek to calm my Sequence, Intensify my Precision and Technical Reasoning, and Tether my Confluence before my mind threatens to jump overboard.

Intensify

The term Intensify refers to increasing your effort to heighten the intensity with which you would engage a Use As Needed Directional Force in order to accomplish a specific task. Intensify is always directed at those Use As Needed Patterns which fall within the 18-24 range of the LCI Scale Scores. These are the Patterns of your Compass Rose that often are mistaken for doldrums of inactivity. It is this very characteristic that requires you to Intensify or ratchet up this Pattern's use. If you do not Intensify its use, it will remain quietly in the background un-noticed and under-used. When determining whether to Intensify the use of a Use As Needed Pattern, it is important to distinguish whether that Pattern operates near the lower end of the Use As Needed spectrum or at the higher end. If your Directional Force operates closer to the Avoid edge of the Use As Needed continuum, then it remains almost dormant unless awakened. On the other hand, if it operates at the upper edge of the Use As Needed continuum, then it is more actively and readily available for use without a great deal of attention having to be paid to it.

The interesting thing about the Processes we Use As Needed is that they provide a rich set of options for us. These Directional Forces are neither our high-maintenance Processes nor our anchors that tend to weigh us down. They, instead, serve as our ballast, providing a counterbalance, a ballast to the extremes of our Use First and Avoid Processes.

I have two Use As Needed Patterns in my Compass Rose: Precision and Technical Reasoning. In the case of the "itemized list of expenditures in chronological order" portion of the task, I can use my Technical Reasoning (19) to see the value in having these data available from a practical business perspective. Further, I can take heart that I am not being asked to "write a report that identifies and analyses the similarities and differences between the two years of expenditures." Listing means fewer words; using fewer words suits my 21 in Precision just fine. Will I need to increase the use of my Precision a bit to have all the expenditures listed accurately? Yes. But the use of the mental energy I need to do so is nowhere near as exhausting as that required to do this task solely by using my Avoid Sequence Process. My Use As Needed Processes give me respite from the pain of trying to accomplish this task with Sequence alone. They calm my Sequence and coach my Use First Confluence to look for calmer seas.

Tether

The term Tether is applied to those Directional Forces you Use First. These fall into the 25 to 35 LCI Scale Score range. These noisy Processes drive your life and your learning. They dominate the makeup of your Compass Rose and always, always seek to be the captain of your destiny. Not infrequently, people will ask me if it is better to have more or fewer Use First Directional Forces. My response is, "You have what you have." As your Directional Forces formed randomly in your brain-mind interface, some became the dominant lead Processes while others assumed the roles of Use As Needed and Avoid. Unlike our multiple intelligences that we inherit from our gene pool, our Compass Rose of Learning Processes appears not to be determined by genetics but by chance—not unlike our right- and left-handedness.

Whatever your makeup, you sail through life with the Compass that formed, and if that Compass consists of one, two, three, or more Use First Learning Processes, then the Directional Forces that drive your life and learning are just what you need. All you are required to do is learn to make them work for you.

Of course, the challenge of using a combination of Use First Processes in concert with your Avoid and Use As Needed Processes is to do so with intention. In the case of your Use First Processes, the intention is to be on alert for when these more vocal Directional Forces need to be Tethered, that is, pulled back, held down, and restrained from overpowering the sails you have carefully set. Yes, there is such a thing as too much wind in your sails.

Tethering involves addressing those Mental Processes that want to hold sway regardless of the course set or the winds encountered. Often, it is our Use First Processes that bring us out of port self-assured, believing that it will be a smooth sail. Then, when we encounter adversity, it is these same Processes that want to stay the course, even when our Use As Needed Directional Forces are urging caution and midcourse correction. Our Use First Processes announce our confidence. The difficulty is that these Processes do not represent competence. Their confidence is sometimes misplaced! Thus, Tethering them helps us gain perspective by communicating with our entire Compass Rose. This is truly a sign of our maturity and our mastery of the skills to navigate our life successfully.

For example, if we can return again to the case of the itemized list of expenditures and apply the tool of Tethering, I find that in my case, where my Use First Process is Confluence at a level of 33, I would naturally ignore the required list-and-compare requirement, writing it off in my mind as a dull way to identify the change that has or has not occurred. Left un-Tethered, my Confluence would then lead me to compare one or two of the major expenditures but not all and would represent the comparison in a figurative rather than literal form. Because either approach would fall short of the expectations for the assignment, I might be perceived as a fool, a slacker, or an incompetent.

Because none of these are what I want to be seen as by my colleagues, I will Tether my Confluence, develop a comparative chart, run it by someone with higher Precision and Sequence than I, and then, having made their suggested changes, submit the report in a timely fashion.

Never Underestimate the Costs

FITing your Directional Forces to a task can cause a major energy drain. The task at hand must be carefully and accurately Decoded. The amount of resources needed to accomplish the task needs to be carefully assessed. Never discount the logistical Mental Resources needed to accomplish the task. Give yourself the space emotionally, mentally, and physically to FIT your Compass Rose to the task. Build in opportunities to regenerate your energy if you have been Tethering or Forging your Compass Patterns for hours at a time. Yet even taking into consideration the amount of energy required to Decode and FIT the task before you, never underestimate the tremendous feeling of accomplishment that awaits you when you have succeeded in completing a task to a degree that you have not achieved before. And never ever leave port without the knowledge of these three tools: Forge, Intensify, and Tether. They are the rudder to navigating uncharted waters.

Staying the Course in Uncharted Waters

Knowing your Compass Rose equips you with the tools and the responsibility to overcome the fear of uncharted waters. Using your Compass Rose and your knowledge of how to Decode and FIT your Learning Processes to a given situation, you are ready to push back the fear and concerns that lie in uncharted waters.

- Don't let the situation control you.
- Don't let fear control you.
- Don't arrive under-resourced.
- Don't arrive without Personal Strategies.

After Decoding and strategizing how to FIT your Patterns to the task, you are wise to use your knowledge of your Compass Rose to develop personal strategies to direct your efforts. The most efficient way to do this is to develop a personal Directional Forces Strategy Card. (See Figure 5.7.) The card consists of the Scale Scores of your four Directional Forces, a Decoding of each aspect of the task at hand, and specific suggestions or strategies for how to use your Directional Forces with Intention by FITING them to the task.

Figure 5.7 Sample Personal Directional Forces Strategy Card

	SEQUENCE	PRECISION	TECHNICAL REASONING	CONFLUENCE
Your LCI Scale Scores	28	15	25	23
Your Own Description of Your Directional Forces:				
How do you 'naturally' use each of your Directional Forces? (Look at your Personal Learning Profile for the descriptions asked for here)	I'm organized. I break my work into steps. I check my work to make sure that I'm following the directions.	I don't ask many questions. I don't read much either. I can find facts when I need to, but I don't use big words, and I hate writing.	What is the purpose of this? How will I ever use it? Let me get my hands on something real and fix it or make it work.	I have some ideas that connect to what I read and that I can use but I am not into taking risks!
Your Analysis of the Directional Forces Needed to Complete the Task (See the Decoded Task Directions):				
What does the assigned task require each of your Directional Forces to do? (Look at the decoded task and determine each Process being required.)	The directions are vague. The time frame is unclear, as are the goals.	Big problem here. The training materials are thick and dense with words. Few illustrations or graphics.	The info is overwhelming in amount, but relevant. This is a must do!	Nothing tricky or different. Risks required.
Your Strategies for Using Your Directional Forces Effectively:				
How can you Forge, Intensify, or Tether your Directional Forces to complete the task successfully?	Establish specific steps based upon how I completed a similar task. Set a clear personal goal and time for completion.	Divide the reading into digestible segments. Draw diagrams of how one piece of info relates to another. Write down new terms.	No strategy card needed. I can make this work!	No strategy needed. I am comfortable with the low risk of this.

You are more effective when you develop a Strategy Card for each major task or assignment. You are even more effective when you complete a logistical analysis and a strategic plan based on your FIT review. In doing so, you become more disciplined to put forth intentional, focused effort. At that point, the uncharted seas are nowhere near as formidable.

Recording the strategies you used to achieve success disciplines you to put forth intentional, focused effort. Developing a Strategy Card requires you to *invest,* not avoid, and *dig deeper* rather than skim the surface of the task at hand. Using a Strategy Card keeps you grounded in using your Compass Rose at all times. After all, your Compass Rose is your greatest asset.

Transferring the Learning

Just as Decoding and FITing Directional Forces to a specific task equips an individual, so does the application of these tools in business and corporate teams. Your Compass Rose of Learning is a powerful tool for navigating difficult situations. The power of using your Compass Rose lies in its ability to develop and/or enhance communication between you and those with whom you live and work. Using the Learning Processes of your Compass Rose identified by the LCI, you can begin a conversation about leading, learning, and working as a team that opens insights into how others use their Compass Roses of Mental Processes to complete their tasks.

With this informed understanding, leaders can guide individuals to Decode challenging team assignments and then direct them with intention to complete the task successfully. Within two weeks of understanding one's Compass Rose, students as young as fifth grade can begin to employ these Personalized Learning Strategies with minimal coaching from their teacher. College students can employ these navigational tools to chart their responses to course assignments within days of identifying their Directional Learning Forces.

At the heart of the process lies the central focus—to develop an ability to describe and explain how their Mental Processes operate as they complete any task. When you can do this, you can identify the disconnection, thereby allowing others to help you understand its source as well as how to overcome it. When we know what comprises the Directional Forces of our Compass Rose, and when we are able to articulate how they operate within us, then leaders, supervisors, friends, colleagues, and even spouses no longer need to be mind readers. The knowledge of our internal Compass Roses provides us with a language to articulate our concerns, to analyze specific tasks, to identify specific problem-solving strategies, and to achieve a successful outcome even in the face of uncharted waters.

Boxing the Compass

- The logistics of your learning allow you to Decode, analyze, and deliver "just in time resources" to any given situation.
- The use of personalized learning strategies allows you to navigate uncharted waters by positioning your Compass Rose to stay the course.
- The challenge of staying the course includes organizational and personal awareness of the True North and Compass Roses of all team members.

Taking Stock

- Choose an upcoming task that you feel might be difficult for you. Use the tool of Decoding and the Word Wall (See Figure 5.3.) to analyze the task. Examine how understanding your Directional Forces of Learning Processes helps you better understand and plan for the task.
- Think about a time when you were less successful in completing an assignment than you wanted to be. How could you have used the strategic tool of FITing to have more successfully completed the task?
- Select an upcoming assignment that is important to you. Using your knowledge of your Compass Rose, develop a personal Directional Forces Strategy Card. (Use the guide and information found in Figure 5.8 and Figure 5.9 to help you complete this task.) Were you able to identify strategies that you would not have used before understanding your Compass Rose?

Figure 5.8 Personal Directional Forces Strategy Card

	SEQUENCE	PRECISION	TECHNICAL REASONING	CONFLUENCE
Your LCI Scale Scores				
Your Own Description of Your Directional Forces:				
How do you 'naturally' use each of your Directional Forces? (Look at your Personal Learning Profile for the descriptions asked for here)				
Your Analysis of the Directional Forces Needed to Complete the Task (See the Decoded Task Directions):				
What does the assigned task require each of your Directional Forces to do? (Look at the decoded task and determine each Process being required.)				
Your Strategies for Using Your Directional Forces Effectively:				
How can you Forge, Intensify, or Tether your Directional Forces to complete the task successfully?				

Figure 5.9 Worksite Strategies

Strategies for the Use of Sequence

If your score in Sequence is between 25 and 35 and you need to Tether it:
- Don't over-analyze each word of the directions. Select and decode the key words focusing on their specific order and the specific deadline.
- Don't over-plan. Leave enough time for double-checking your work before sending or submitting it.

If your score in Sequence is between 7 and 17 and you need to Forge it:
- Use what you learned from an earlier experience to help you understand the directions and expectations for this new assignment.
- Clear your mind, focus like a laser beam, and allow no interruptions until you have completed the task from beginning to end.

If your score in Sequence is between 18 and 24, use some of the above strategies selecting those that match the specific Directional Forces of your Compass Rose.

Strategies for the Use of Precision

If your score in Precision is between 25 and 35 and you need to Tether it:
- Read what you need carefully, once—then go on.
- Accept that you won't have a flawless result the first time, but you will have an excellent product worthy of further refinement.

If your score in Precision is between 7 and 17 and you need to Forge it:
- Coach yourself to read the information in front of you and record key points.
- Identify key terms that ask for important facts or details then check your work for accuracy.

If your score in Precision is between 18 and 24, use some of the above strategies selecting those that match the specific Directional Forces of your Compass Rose.

Strategies for the Use of Technical Reasoning

If your score in Technical Reasoning is between 25 and 35 and you need to Tether it:
• Think of each project, task or assignment as a machine that you are required to make operational.
• Force yourself to translate your thoughts into words and diagrams as a means of presenting your work, being careful to explain and label the parts and their function so that you do not present your product as disjointed pieces of undeveloped thought.

If your score in Technical Reasoning is between 7 and 17 and you need to Forge it:
• Identify the purpose and relevance of the task at hand, then
• Resolve that this is a problem you can tackle through the use of reading and following directions (Precision and Sequence) and through relying on your first-hand life experiences to model how to approach this challenge.

If your score in Technical Reasoning is between 18 and 24, use some of the above strategies selecting those that match the specific Directional Forces of your Compass Rose.

Strategies for the Use of Confluence

If your score in Confluence is between 25 and 35 and you need to Tether it:
• Don't create your own version of what you have been asked to produce. Decode it as stated and respond as expected not as you might prefer to complete the project.
• Remember that others may need help seeing how your idea connects to the task at hand. Be patient and professional in explaining or graphically representing the big picture.

If your score in Confluence is between 7 and 17 and you need to Forge it:
• Plan a new approach, a small risk that allows you to experience both the security of planning and the adventure of trying something new.
• Identify a change that you would like to explore and implement over time once you are well informed and prepared for it. Then begin the journey!

If your score in Confluence is between 18 and 24, use some of the above strategies selecting those that match the specific Directional Forces of your Compass Rose.

Insights

6. Assuming the Helm for Success

"The basis for leadership is learning, and
principally learning from experience."
—Warren Bennis
Distinguished Professor of Business

The Focus

- Taking the helm
- Detaching barnacles for smoother sailing

It's now time to don your captain's hat and navigate your life with intention. As you are piped aboard your vessel, you think of William Henley's famous poem, "Invictus," which boldly declares, "I am the master of my fate, I am the captain of my soul."

At this point, you might find yourself pausing and asking yourself, "Am I really ready for this responsibility?" Clearly, navigating your life is no small task. The preceding chapters suggest that the successful navigation of our lives requires identifying our True North and familiarizing ourselves with our Compass Roses of Directional Learning Forces.

Now, as you prepare to put your hands on the helm and navigate your life with this new awareness of self, you will want to do some final preparations. Begin by first checking the following:

- Have you charted your course relying on your True North?
- Do you have your Personal Compass Rose at the ready?
- Are all metacognitive hands on deck?

If the answer to each of these questions is "yes," then you are almost ready to weigh anchor. One critical action needs to occur first, however, and that is doing one last walk-around to make sure your vessel is seaworthy. Primarily, is the ship water-tight, scraped of barnacles, and fit for service?

In other words, are you prepared to detach from your old behaviors and execute your new awareness, knowing the challenges you will face? Are you willing to identify behaviors and responses that have become unconscious habits, and replace them by staying in the moment and charting your course? Are you ready to base your actions, not on the way you have always done it, but on your awareness of your Compass Rose and the potential this awareness holds to navigate a familiar situation in a new, more effective course? Most important, are you ready to allow your Compass Rose to direct you and your Metacognitive Team to transcend any of your human frailties?

I emphasize this point because I believe we often embark on a new venture without preparing ourselves to recognize that when we seek to change, we take our old selves with us. We take our old habits, behaviors, and personal learning history! Nothing is left behind. So be aware that knowing your Compass Rose and using it with intention to navigate your life will not remove life's obstacles. It won't make your life a glassy sea. There will be an initial discomfort as you learn to use your Compass Rose with intention; there will be a temporary lag in action as you learn to FIT your Directional Forces to the task and communicate with your metacognitive crew.

However, none of these transition costs outweighs the benefits you gain by knowing your Compass Rose. None compares to the freeing experience you feel when you navigate your life by using the newly acquired knowledge of your learning self, able to FIT the charting of your course to the seas that lie before you! Little is more powerful than knowing that you can draw upon your crew of Metacognitive Processes, your personal learning team, to complete tasks successfully that formerly magnified your "barnacles" and kept you from achieving success.

Barnacles and Your Ship's Seaworthiness

You may not know nor be particularly interested in the life and economic issues involving barnacles, but the barnacle serves as a sound metaphor for the types of behaviors that can hold you back from making your vessel seaworthy. So I ask your indulgence as I seek in these next few paragraphs to draw some parallels between the common frailties of our human makeup and that of the sea crustacean, the barnacle.

To the barnacle's credit, it uses one of the strongest natural adhesives known to science to stick to rocks, wood, and, yes, ship bottoms. "These unassuming creatures have the remarkable ability to stick themselves in the midst of rushing water on the propellers and hulls of ocean-going ships, at the mouths of huge water intake pipes, and along the water line of supertankers," notes Robert Baier, professor and director of the Industry/University Center for Biosurfaces at the State University of New York (SUNY) Buffalo (Baier & Meyer, 1992, p. 166).

Most interesting, Baier explains, "The glues that hold these very different animals in place are virtually identical. Nature has devised a method for producing this ultimate superglue and conserved it across species. If chemists could make a synthetic version, it might be the ideal bonding material for medical devices designed to be placed inside the human body." Interestingly, barnacles, those little beasties of the sea, can play a dual role: In the first case, they pose a real problem for shipping; while in the second case, they could advance medical science by providing insights into superadhesive technology.

"Well," you might be thinking, "how much of an impact can these little creatures have on something as large as a seaworthy vessel?" Actually, the accumulation of barnacles can slow ships and reduce their maneuverability. In fact, "of the $550 million to $600 million the Navy spends annually on powering its ships and submarines, at least $50 million stems directly from drag because of marine growth fouling the vessels' hulls," confirms an environmental quality program officer in the Office of Naval Research's (2001) physical science division. Barnacles pose no small problem to navigation!

Similarly, personal barnacles are no small problem to our ability to maneuver and navigate our lives! They affect our maneuverability; they slow down our change process; and they weigh on our minds. If not confronted, "scraped," and removed, they can inhibit the successful navigation of our lives. The story that follows illustrates this point.

The Story

Captain Bob (Dr. Robert Grandin)

I met Bob in Greece. We were both attending an international conference on learning and instruction. He came to my presentation on Learning Processes and approached me immediately afterward. "This is what I have been doing with students at my school," he said. "But I've had no language, no terms by which to call it. This is fabulous, just fabulous." And so began the tale of my journey with Bob.

Now, from the outset, it is important for the reader to know that I have Bob's permission to tell this tale, and I remain a colleague of Bob's even though thousands of miles separate us. I share his story because it is one of a person vested in knowing and understanding his Compass Rose, but not always employing it as comprehensibly as he might.

Bob hails from Australia. He is a nationally recognized hero of the Battle of Long Tan, a decorated Air Force helicopter pilot in Viet Nam, a math teacher, an author, a sheep rancher, a cattle farmer, a school administrator, a shop owner, a consultant, a university instructor, and a husband, father, and grandfather. (The last, I believe, is the highest source of his pride.)

Bob is a *Strong-willed Learner*. He uses three Use First Directional Forces to lead his life. He Avoids none. For over 60 years, Bob has intuitively navigated his life journey using his Use First Precision, Use First Technical Reasoning, and Use First Confluence. Bob is a dyed-in-the-wool one-man team.

Bob has had his successes in life and his failures. He would attribute both to his Strong-willed use of his Compass Rose. Bob's True North involves freeing himself and others to experience the fullness of life without the labels and limitations placed by traditional education. He is committed to making a difference to that end. He is determined to grow further in one area: developing the navigational skills and the discipline to FIT his Processes to those with whom he is working when the situation calls for it.

At one point, Bob came to the United States and worked with me at our Let Me Learn, Inc., national center. During that time, he provided various services to teachers of adjudicated youth, intervention teams at a large center for early childhood education, and teachers in a secondary regional school system.

Bob found following office and university procedures some-what taxing. As a result, he simply ignored them. He did not take responsibility for his Use As Needed Sequence to follow procedures but instead made up his own rules. At one point during an annual performance review, he turned to me, his su-pervisor, and said, "Mate, are you concerned that I don't follow your directions?"

I responded, "I'm concerned that you think you are follow-ing some of my directions, but you refuse to ask questions to determine whether you are on the right course. You let your Strong-willedness get in the way of asking for what you need."

Bob countered, "Let me explain something to you. I ran away and joined the Australian Air Force when I was 16. My commanding officer had me in his office for a talk, and it wasn't because he wanted to commend me. He delivered his message, made his point as to why I was in his presence, and then con-cluded, 'Robert, apparently you believe there is only one job in this nation that suits you.'"

Bob said, "I asked him, 'What might that be, sir?'"

"Prime Minister, and that spot is already taken!"

At that point, Bob turned to me and said, "Don't worry if you haven't gotten me to change. It's been over 50 years since I first heard those words. I think they probably still ring true."

So why is Bob "the story" of this chapter? Bob is an exam-ple of someone who lives his life to the fullest, holding fast to the attitude of, "Damn the torpedoes, full speed ahead!" Bob's Strong-willed approach to captaining his life and the lives of those around him involves sweeping up those on his "team" using the skills he learned as a young man playing rugby: fake, trick, dodge, and weave. These also remain the barnacles in his life. Bob never embraced knowing when and how to tack with the winds, using his Compass Rose and knowledge of his Directional Forces to interact and communicate with others as he strives toward his destination. What Bob is still working to develop are the navigational tools of logistics and strategies that can help him temper his Strong-willedness and assuage his Confluent tendencies to live life as an all-or-nothing wager, regardless of its impact on the rest of his crew.

The Learning

As I reflect on Bob's story, I recognize that of all the aspects of *Finding Your Way*, developing strategies to reconfigure the use of your Directional Forces for specific tasks or assignments would be the least appealing to Bob. Why? Bob has chosen not to adjust his Compass of Learning Processes but rather to use them as they are and let the outcomes fall as they may. This approach allows the barnacles to remain attached to Captain Bob's ship.

I think, at this point, it is vital to reveal that when I approached Bob about using his story to illustrate the challenge of removing barnacles before trying to set sail, he graciously consented. "It is always difficult to read things that come close to the bone," he noted. "I am also happy to recognize that this is my Achilles' heel. I can only explain that when you see immediately a solution, you often do not listen to the way others see the solution. I hope that by telling my story it helps others to recognize the point that understanding Personal Learning

Processes, our Compass Rose, as you call it, can help each of us find our way to more productive learning and working with others."

There is no doubt. The requirements for finding your way involve engagement, execution, discipline, and detachment. Finding your way demands a commitment to review your Personal Learning Journey and identify your True North; a dedication to use your navigational tools of Decoding, strategizing, and FITing to navigate the charted and uncharted waters of your life; the discipline of detachment to begin the separation from old behaviors (our frailties of habit); and the steadfastness to achieve a state of proficiency and to come safe home.

Scraping Away the Frailties From Our Vessel: The Barnacles of Our Personal and Professional Lives

The Excuse Barnacle

The excuse barnacle thrives in an environment where persons use their Compass Roses to make excuses for their behavior. They do not invest energy in listening carefully, following directions, or completing tasks as assigned. The Compass Rose of their Directional Forces becomes an excuse for noncompliance and slipshod work. They may say, "Oh, you know I don't understand directions. Just look at my level of Sequence. It's a glaring Avoid!"

Once you scrape away the excuses, you, as captain of your ship, now recognize that knowing your Directional

Forces provides an explanation, not an excuse. Regardless of what constitutes your Compass Rose, you are responsible for using it to make life work. The point of *Finding Your Way* is just that. Know your True North, understand your Compass Rose, and make life work for you because you are now well equipped with your knowledge and logistical and strategic tools to do so.

The SMTDSLT Barnacle

A particularly aggressive barnacle is the SMTDSLT (pronounced Smitd-Slit) standing for "So much to do; so little time." Of all the various species of personal barnacles, this one is the most debilitating. As the diseases of scurvy and beriberi ravaged the health of sailors in the eighteenth century, SMTDSLT ravages the life-space of most in the 21st century. The SMTDSLT barnacle attacks your vessel, attaching itself one layer at a time using this weighty rationale:

> Navigating life is a great concept, and it is very intriguing, *but* I *don't have time* for visiting my Personal Learning Journey *right now*. *Once* I *have* this important *project done, then* I can consider visiting my Learning Journey and developing my Personal Compass Rose. *Until then,* I just need to keep doing what I am doing the best I know how. *Later* I can take time for myself. *Right now*, I have work, family, schedules, obligations, responsibilities.

SMTDSLT literally brings people to a standstill and holds them captive in their layers of to-do lists, text messages, e-mails, and phone messages. It subsumes all personal time and personal space. It layers them in barnacles of overscheduled and overwhelmed. They remain what one author calls, "CrazyBusy" (Hallowell, 2007). The current infestation of this species is not a new phenomenon.

While doing the research for this book, I came across a comment made by Louisa May Alcott, the 19th century American writer who created *Little Women,* and who modern scholarship is rediscovering as a fascinating and original thinker. Her thoughts remain applicable today:

> When I had youth I had no money; now I have the money I have no time; and when I get the time, if I ever do, I shall have no health to enjoy life. I suppose it's the discipline I need; but it's rather hard to love the things I do, and see them go by because duty chains me to my galley (Saxton, 1977, p. 337).

The SDTSLT barnacle has a long history. There is never enough time in life to do all that you want to do in an hour, a day, a week, a month, or a year.

To avoid this conundrum, you will need to consider how you can scrape off the invasive SMDTSLT barnacle. Begin by revisiting your navigational tools and making your Strategy Card to get through various time-crunch situations. Then use your logistics of Decoding, and the strategic use of FITing your Patterns, to arrive at task completion more efficiently.

One thing to note is that practicing the use of your navigational tools expands your ability to respond to all types of situations. The regular and intentional use of your Compass Rose will help you find your bearings and help you navigate a course equipped with insights and understandings of self that go far beyond the surface to the heart of your human essence—your learning self.

Staying the Course: Taking the Helm

You will know that you have arrived at a state of significant proficiency when you can't think about setting out on a course of action without using the concepts and constructs of your personal learning self to steer your personal and professional navigational course to success and fulfillment.

People who only keep the knowledge of their Compass Roses at surface level, using it only at parties to impress or as an excuse for not doing their assigned work, significantly underestimate its power to enhance and develop their personal and professional selves. The fact that Captain Bob, the character of this chapter's story, shared this sentiment suggests that he has clearly begun to use the very tools he earlier had dismissed. It is apparent to me from his response to my query for permission to tell his story that he has taken on the responsibility of *Finding His Way* to achieve the state of having his Compass Rose deeply embedded in his professional and daily life.

Assuming the Helm in Calm Seas or Stormy

Having set your course, Boxed your Compass, and made your ship seaworthy, you are prepared to take the helm. Please be aware that in assuming this responsibility you are the same-different person you were before. You will possess the same intelligences, the same interests, and the same idiosyncrasies as those you had before *Finding Your Way*, but now, you know how to navigate life more efficiently and effectively. You understand how to use your Directional Forces and your navigational tools. You are prepared for the personal and professional change in perspective and motivation that is about to occur within you. In many ways, this knowledge allows you to feel unbounded. You are emancipated from the labels and judgments you have experienced along your life journey. You are equipped to remove the barnacles of unproductive behavior. You are prepared to use your metacognitive team to overcome your individual frailty. You are ready to assume responsibility in a manner that you have not been prepared to do so before. You are prepared to set the course and stay the course.

Boxing the Compass

- As captain of my learning vessel, I need to execute my new awareness while detaching from old behaviors.
- Assuming the helm requires me to ready myself for the sea change ahead.

Taking Stock

Confronting the Unknown

- Keep a brief, running record this week of how you are interacting with the various tasks or topics confronting you at work and at home. Pay particular attention to how you respond to your SMTDSLT barnacle.
- Review the situational excuses listed below. Then identify how you could use your Compass Rose and the Navigational Tools of Decoding, FITing, and Personal Strategies to address each:
  - I am not prepared, equipped, or experienced enough to do anything about the situation.
  - I don't see why others are concerned about this situation, so why should I be concerned and waste my time and energy?
  - I don't have sufficient information to make a determination as to what to do.
  - I don't want to risk making a mistake and losing others' respect or friendship, or my professional/financial status.

Insights

PART III

FINDING YOUR WAY:
SAFE HOME!

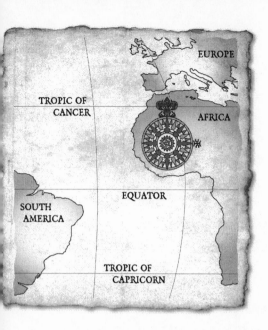

7. Navigating the Flat World of the 21st Century

"I am no longer afraid of storms, for I
am learning to sail my own ship."

—Louisa May Alcott
Work: A Story of Experience

The Focus

- Identifying the learning challenges facing you in the 21st century
- Understanding how you can use the Directional Forces of your Compass Rose to navigate a "flat" world

This final chapter of *Finding Your Way* focuses on how to use your Directional Forces to learn faster and more effectively. Specifically, this chapter seeks to prepare you to navigate the "flat" world in which you live and work.

The term "flat world" was coined by Thomas Friedman (2005) in his book *The World is Flat, A Brief History of the 21st Century*. In it, he describes the dramatic changes taking place in the global marketplace because of the new technological platforms of the 21st century.

Friedman writes:

> it is now possible for more people than ever to collaborate and compete in real time with more other people on more different kinds of work from more different corners of the planet and on a more equal footing than at any previous time in the history of the world—using computers, e-mail, networks, teleconferencing, and dynamic new software (p. 6).

"It's difficult to argue against such a declaration," you say, "but how do advancements in technological platforms connect with my rate of learning—or my children's, for that matter?"

Simply put, the faster the world connects, the faster learning needs to occur to keep pace. The faster the new technology platforms, the faster your mind needs to learn and adapt. Now more than ever, you need to be able to use your Compass Rose to navigate the world in which you find yourself.

The frontier to be conquered is no longer found on this planet or even in the space that surrounds it. The challenge of the 21st century is the reduced amount of time between stimulus and response, between e-mail and response, and between text message and response. The shrinkage of space affects the quality of communication in the flat world. No miles between neighbors. No walls between nations. No distance between cause and effect. Now instant messaging, the Internet, cell phones, and 24-hour satellite surveillance have flattened the world, bringing information resources within our immediate grasp. Along with the increase in these resources has come the abundance of communication that allows little or no downtime for problem solving, weighing choices, or considering pros and cons. Instant comment, instant reaction; instant problem, instant solution.

In the flat landscape of the 21st century, we no longer have the luxury of time to wait to see if things work out. Instead, we are required to be immediately responsive. We are required to get it faster than we have ever gotten it before. We are called on to communicate more quickly and more effectively. Every word we say or write is instantly posted, blogged about, and scrutinized. The issue becomes one of communicating with greater awareness of the recipient of the message, while at the same time needing to communicate faster and more efficiently.

The landscape of business communication for the 21st century has changed, and our mindscapes must be ready to meet the challenge. Campbell's comment in the Foreword of this book, speaking clearly to this point, reminds us of the retooling our understanding of learning will need to undergo if we intend to increase our achievement in the 21st century: "Success in to-day's global environment will depend on how well people can learn and apply new ideas and skills effectively." Chief among those skills is communication. The convergence of our global landscape with the mindscape within each of us only serves to heighten the challenge of communication. That challenge is the focus of the story of this final chapter.

The Story

This story is about a process. It is based on an actual corporate experience that represents an all-too-common occurrence in business and industry—communication disconnection. In this particular case, two groups of engineers, located 12 hundred miles apart, have been given the task of moving the production of a chemical product from a research lab on the East Coast of the United States to a production plant located in the Midwest.

For months, the East Coast research team developed and scaled the process for the manufacture of a new product, experimenting and problem solving until it achieved the desired outcome. When it was time for the Midwest group to begin the manufacturing process, the two groups talked by teleconference to have the alignment go smoothly. Twenty-first century technology made the 12-hundred-mile separation shrink to the size of a single room.

The disconnection in communication began—not at the point of the actual telecommunication nor as the individual

team members reported the steps necessary to align the production process—but much earlier. It began when the East
Coast research team failed to identify and address its Learning
Processes and those of the manufacturing team with whom it
was seeking to communicate.

The East Coast team was well prepared to tell the other
team the procedures it had used to achieve the high standards
of quality it sought to produce. The exchange was sequenced
and very detailed, as the one team related to the other the "end
knowledge" it had gained during its scale experience. It did so
primarily using its Precision. However, it wasn't until several
telecommunication conferences later that the teams' supervisor
realized that the information the East Coast team was communicating was not helping the Midwest team achieve its goal.
What seemed like a simple hand off of information turned out
to be much more complicated!

Had both teams begun their teleconference by explaining the Learning Processes of those participating in the conference, they could have avoided both frustration and loss
of time. Knowing that the average scores of the two teams'
Patterns were significantly different in Precision and Technical
Reasoning would have been a clear advantage to both teams.

Average Learning Connections Inventory
(LCI) Scale Scores of the Team Members

	Sequence	Precision	Technical	Confluence
East Coast	24	27	23	24
Midwest	23	22	28	23

Considering the average Learning Patterns of each team would have helped them prepare for their professional interaction and exchange of information. Had they developed learning-based communication strategies for talking with each other before the teleconferences, they could have cut through the communication barrier and interacted more efficiently and effectively.

The reason for the failure to reach an efficient hand off lies in the way the hand off was communicated. In this particular case, the Midwest manufacturing team was missing essential pieces of information, such as the history of the problems that arose during development of the initial scale processes. The East Coast team, when developing the process, had run into numerous problems and had worked through them; however, when doing the hand off, it never mentioned the issues it had encountered—much less how those issues had been resolved or reconciled during the course of the scale process. The East Coast team relied on its Use First Precision and Use as Needed Technical Reasoning and assumed, because the problems had been solved, why rehash them?

In addition to failing to communicate this vital information, the East Coast team also failed to tell what it had done to *address* the problems as they arose. Clearly, there were things the East Coast team had learned during its scale phase that were recorded at the time, but not included in its hand off directions. The East Coast team assumed that because it had already overcome these problems, relating them at this point was irrelevant.

Meanwhile, the Midwest production team did not *ask* about the various problems it was encountering during the scale. Instead, the Midwest team was busy using its collective Technical Reasoning to solve what it thought were new problems. The Midwest team never suspected that "the devil was in the details" that had been omitted by the East Coast team. Because its collective use of Precision was only Use As Needed, the Midwest team failed to delve deeper into what finally led the East Coast team to a successful product scale.

Gradually, the two teams became aware that even though their members had written the most precise and accurate directions and carefully explained them in detail, the teams should not have assumed that the members of the other team, reading or hearing those directions, would be able to produce the same product as the members giving the directions. In this case, it became evident that giving *end-state* details, without revisiting the details of the problem solving encountered during the journey to the final answer, did not fully communicate *how* to achieve the intended outcome. Both teams used their engineering skills well, but one team relied too much on Precision while the other focused on problem solving using its Technical Reasoning, and failed to use sufficient Precision to inquire about the problems encountered and solved during the scale process.

As the outcome of this story suggests, without being aware of your Directional Learning Forces and of those with whom you are communicating, you are likely to experience a disconnection in communication. What both teams learned was that knowing the Learning Processes of each other and then using their own Learning Processes with intention was vital to communicating with one another. They also learned that communicating effectively was essential to achieving a successful hand-off.

What *you* can learn from this story is that if you use your Learning Processes with intention, you can achieve more effective communication. No 21st-century technology can replace the most sophisticated technology—the mind. The mind remains the most vital technology for communicating with others and, thereby, for navigating your professional work life even in the flat world of our 21st century.

The Learning

Navigating the world of the 21st century requires high-speed learning and communicating. Without the intentional use of your Learning Processes, you will find this difficult to do. Friedman's (2006) words make the challenge clear: "The first, and most important, ability you can develop in a flat world is the ability to learn how to learn" (p. 302). Further, Friedman explains that "the society that has the strength of sound governance, the innovation of technology, and the ability to *learn* [emphasis added] will be the one that continues to succeed and achieve." The "flattened world" brings with it the challenge for us to understand one another and to communicate and interact with one another at an ever-increasing speed. Again and again, we are reminded of the central role the use of our minds, our True North, and our Compass Rose plays in our achieving success in the 21st century.

More than two decades ago, Neil Postman (1990), chair of the Department of Culture and Communications at New York University, speaking in Berlin before an international conference of the world's finest minds in the high-tech industry, made some extraordinary predictions about technology and its long-term effects on global society. His premise was that knowing information faster and more completely did not ensure faster, more complete communication. He based his conviction on his knowledge of how the invention of the printing press almost five hundred years earlier had ushered in the age of information overload. Because of Gutenberg's invention, we find ourselves flooded with the printed word. And now the revolution ushered in by Gutenberg has gone one crucial step further: Even when we seek to go paperless, we are confronted with the 21st century technology that results in our desktops being flooded with e-mails, instant messaging, and attachments! The world of information now knows no borders, has no limits, and operates with few restrictions.

The point Postman makes is that modern technology has affected not just the amount but the *quality* of human communication. Knowing your Directional Forces helps you understand how the amount of information you receive daily can affect both your internal thought processes and your external ability to communicate. Internally, your mind is inundated with words and data. You find yourself with no time to think, reason, and respond appropriately. Externally, your professional world inundates you with wave upon wave of information. You find yourself sinking under its weight, unable to bail fast enough, to delegate and channel it quickly enough, to keep yourself afloat. The speed with which information is communicated leaves you with little time to establish its *context*, little time to process it, and even less time to discern its implications. Communicating effectively under these circumstances is stressful at best, and impossible at worst.

The Technology of Learning

The technology that operates the "flat world" is powerful; the technology of learning is more powerful. It is powerful because it is universal. Every individual, regardless of geographic location, race, color, or class has the capacity to learn. Learning, however, is not just global; it is personal! The technology of the mind that fuels learning is powerful because it is central to our individual personhood. It defines who we are and how we behave; it defines how others perceive us and interact with us; it develops our capacity and molds our future. In every individual is a system for learning that is not only individual—it is very personal.

Across the globe, the technology of the Learning Processes of our mind, the Directional Forces that compose our Compass Rose, provides the means by which our consciousness, our awareness of self, equips us to learn. Learning is universal. Learning is individual. Learning is very personal. When we know our True North and the Directional Forces of our Compass Rose of Learning Processes, we can meet the challenge of the flat world head-on. Using our minds with intention, we can navigate the flat world.

With knowledge of our Learning Processes, we can take time to Mull and Connect and Rehearse *before* we hit the send button on our computer. We can become more articulate in expressing our thoughts when speaking or writing because we have taken the time to analyze the Learning Processes of the recipient of our communication. We can build team time to do intentional Assessing, Reflecting, and Revisiting to weigh the information in the balance and check to see if it aligns with our previous experience.

With knowledge of our Directional Learning Processes, we can communicate more effectively in the flat world. For example, we can acknowledge and strategically address the Precision of information that otherwise would overwhelm us with details and annoy us with its lack of relevance. We can participate in meetings and not be inundated with myriads of ideas from a group leader who Uses Confluence First. We can develop personal strategies to communicate our thoughts—with intention—to others who might otherwise be puzzled by our lack of Sequence and what they might see as our tendency toward scatteredness and lack of organization.

Clearly, what is required of us as citizens of the 21st-century global community is to use our minds, our Compass Roses, and our learning tools with ever greater and greater intention to understand and communicate with others.

The Challenge of Navigating Your Life in the 21st Century

The greatest challenge of the 21st century remains the same challenge that faced Harrison, Einstein, and, yes, our grandparents and parents:

- To recognize the True North of your life.
- To acknowledge and use the Compass Rose of learning in you.

The key difference between those of earlier days and you is that you now have the technology to understand your learning self and can use that technology to navigate your life. You have an Advanced Learning System that can assist you in understanding and using your Compass Rose of Directional Learning Processes with intention to succeed in life.

You do not need to begin your learning journey ill equipped. Using your True North as the reference point and the Directional Forces of your Compass Rose, you can explore, discover, and plot your life course so that, regardless of your destination, you can be assured that you can *set your course, stay the course, and come safe home*! To you, the reader, I would add, "Godspeed."

Boxing the Compass

- One challenge facing individuals and corporations in the 21st-century global community is to learn how to learn ever more effectively and efficiently.
- A second challenge facing individuals and corporations in the 21st-century global community is to understand how to navigate their futures in an ever-flattening world.

Taking Stock

- As someone prepared to navigate your life by relying on a richer understanding of your learning self, you may want to launch your next task or project by creating a personal development plan to guide your effort.

- Begin by selecting an area of your life where you would like to feel a greater sense of fulfillment or satisfaction, a greater sense of efficiency and effectiveness.

- Identify one or two specific things in your control that you would like to change to achieve greater success with that aspect of your life.

- Develop an individually tailored series of experiences focused specifically on addressing the change you want to bring about.

- Then, using the chart provided to set your course, track the progress of your course, and achieve the change goal you have set to navigate by using your knowledge of your learning self effectively and efficiently.

Figure 7.2 My Personal Chart for Navigating the Flat World

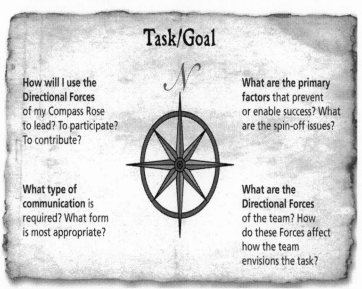

Task/Goal

How will I use the Directional Forces of my Compass Rose to lead? To participate? To contribute?

What are the primary factors that prevent or enable success? What are the spin-off issues?

What type of communication is required? What form is most appropriate?

What are the Directional Forces of the team? How do these Forces affect how the team envisions the task?

Insights

THE REPRISE

"I'm doing what I think I was put on this earth to do. And I'm really grateful to have something that I'm passionate about and that I think is profoundly important."

—Marian Wright Edelman
Children's Defense Fund

The Reprise: "Are We There Yet?"

The nationally syndicated radio commentator, Paul Harvey, used to share a story each day, dividing it into two segments. In the first segment, he would capture the listener's attention and bring the listener to a critical point in the story only to stop to read an ad. After the commercial, Harvey would return to the air with the dramatic line, "And now, the *rest* of the story."

The story included here in the Reprise is intended to do exactly the same: tell the rest of the story that began in Chapter 1. As you may recall, that story ends with, "My journey does not end here. Over the past 15 years, I have learned how to find my way more efficiently and effectively because I have learned to understand how my Directional Learning Processes work. Even more important, I have learned how to use these Processes with intention."

My, "and now the rest of the story," picks up at that exact point. Determined to understand myself and the adult students with whom I was working better, I enlisted a number of graduate students and colleagues to help study the disconnection between what we taught and what our students actually carried into their personal and professional lives.

We studied 100 professional educational managers, supervisors, and chief school administrators over a period of six months. The single common denominator found in each case was the following: *How* one learns—not *what* one learns—is the key to understanding what an individual does with coursework after entering the work world. *How* you learn is the single determiner of how much you retain, how well you retain it, and how well you implement *what* is presented to you as professional development or professional training.

After studying these 100 professionals, it became clear that to understand the success or failure of getting the content across we needed first and foremost to understand the Directional Learning Forces of those whom we were teaching and how those Learning Forces blended or conflicted with our own. Having arrived at this insight, we felt driven to continue to explore more fully what drew them off course and, thereby, limited their ability to navigate their work world once they left the harbor of professional studies. Based on what we learned from this initial study, we devoted the next fourteen years to learning the following by working in various professional and career contexts:

- Each human has the potential to learn. Therefore, we are to value and respect their lives by equipping them to use their talents and learning abilities with intention.
- Individuals who actively participate in their personal learning journeys are best equipped to use their learning potential more fully.
- People who are equipped to understand their Directional Forces, their Learning Processes, will use them appropriately to enhance their work, their leadership, and their personal relationships with family, friends, and work associates (Kottkamp & Johnston, 1998; Johnston and Calleja, 2000).

Although our True North helped us strive to maintain the integrity of the research, our collective Directional Forces allowed us sufficient Sequence to understand the need to structure the explanation of learning that we were developing, sufficient Precision to write the theory and record the research outcomes, sufficient Technical Reasoning to solve problems along the way and keep the applications relevant and practical, and sufficient Confluence to take the risk to challenge the status quo of the standard operating procedures of schooling, training, and professional development that confronted us.

It is this work, completed with over 50,000 individuals during the past 15 years, that has resulted in the development of an Advanced Learning System known as the Let Me Learn Process®, a registered trademarked system that informs and prepares you to navigate your learning life.

One More Story

I have still one more story to tell. That story is yours and mine. Strategically positioning ourselves and our organizations for the 21st century begins by strategically positioning ourselves to overcome the challenges we face in all aspects of our lives. Unlike the centuries that have preceded, which focused on unmasking the mysteries of the universe, the monumental yet achievable challenges we face involve identifying the True North of our lives, developing our personal Compass Roses by which to navigate our journeys, and developing the personal strategies that will build our capacity to achieve our highest potential.

That is what brought you to read this book—is it not? We are here because we all want to do more than exist in a mundane world. Each of us wants to do more than just get by. We each are seeking to use our Directional Forces to achieve our True North and to use our Compass Rose to position ourselves to achieve extraordinary accomplishments in the 21st century. What we hold here are powerful tools and a great opportunity to apply them with skill.

But there are things we cannot afford. We cannot afford to abandon our sense of True North and be driven off course by the storms of *isms*—criticism, skepticism, cynicism, and pessimism. Nor can we afford to languish in the doldrums and horse latitudes of quiet acceptance of the status quo. Instead, we must chart our course and stay the course. That is what this book is about. We must continue to explore and discover new territory within our learning selves. We need to use the collaboration of our Directional Forces to drive our dreams, to chart our career courses, and to solve the problems that confront us as individuals as well as the organizations and greater society we seek to serve.

My personal learning journey is no longer the journey of one person. It is now a journey of many. The journey now includes you and me. Using our newly acquired knowledge of our Compass Roses and personal learning tools, we are prepared for the 21st century with powerful navigational tools and many opportunities to apply them and use them with skill. To play on the words of Paul Harvey, *and now you know the best of the story.*

APPENDIX A

LCI

Learning Connections Inventory
Christine A. Johnston
Gary R. Dainton

Name: _____

There are three parts to the Learning Connections Inventory.

- In Part I, you are asked to respond to 28 different statements by selecting your answers from the five choices.
- In Part II, you are asked for a written response to three questions.
- In Part III, you are to place your scores for each answer and tabulate the results

- Feel free to begin with either Part I or Part II.
- After completing Parts I and II, complete Part III.

PART I
Instructions

Next, you will find 28 statements, each followed by five phrases: (1) "Never," (2) "Almost Never," (3) "Sometimes," (4) "Almost Always," and (5) "Always."

Read each statement carefully, and then circle the phrase that best depicts the degree to which the sentence describes how you learn.

Sample Statement

A. I like to demonstrate my knowledge by giving impromptu presentations.

Never   Almost Never   Sometimes   Almost Always   Always

Words of Encouragement: Take the time you need to consider your responses carefully. Although there is no right or wrong answer, there are answers that are more accurate to whom you are than others. Selecting answers from each category provides a more accurate picture of your specific Learning Processes. Choosing answers is not always easy. Often, if you decide on your answer, you will select "Sometimes" as a compromise. Rather than doing this, we encourage you to change the wording in a sentence or add to the wording so that you can select a response from the continuum that specifically describes you. Feel free to write any changes in the booklet. Most important, have fun, relax, and enjoy learning more about yourself.

Professional Workplace Form Adapted for Finding Your Way

1. I prefer tasks where I use mechanical/technical tools and equipment.

   Never   Almost Never   Sometimes   Almost Always   Always

2. I need to have a complete understanding of my work task before I feel comfortable starting an assignment.

   Never   Almost Never   Sometimes   Almost Always   Always

3. I become frustrated when I have to wait patiently for someone to finish giving directions.

   Never   Almost Never   Sometimes   Almost Always   Always

4. I begin any new work assignment by asking questions and gathering background information.

   Never   Almost Never   Sometimes   Almost Always   Always

5. I become frustrated if I am expected to multitask rather than complete one assignment before I am given another.

   Never   Almost Never   Sometimes   Almost Always   Always

6. I prefer to work alone without anyone's supervision or guidance.

Never   Almost Never   Sometimes   Almost Always   Always

7. I pride myself in giving factually correct answers to the questions I am asked.

Never   Almost Never   Sometimes   Almost Always   Always

8. I don't like to do my work in just one way, especially when I have a better idea I would like to try.

Never   Almost Never   Sometimes   Almost Always   Always

9. I automatically take notes whenever I am given instructions on a new task.

Never   Almost Never   Sometimes   Almost Always   Always

10. I clean up my work area as soon as I finish a task.

Never   Almost Never   Sometimes   Almost Always   Always

11. I enjoy the challenge of repairing, making, or building something.

Never   Almost Never   Sometimes   Almost Always   Always

12. I react quickly to questions without spending time thinking through my answers.

Never   Almost Never   Sometimes   Almost Always   Always

13. I am told by others that I am very organized.

Never   Almost Never   Sometimes   Almost Always   Always

14. I ask more questions than most people because I just enjoy knowing things.

Never   Almost Never   Sometimes   Almost Always   Always

15. I like to figure out how equipment and machinery work.

Never   Almost Never   Sometimes   Almost Always   Always

16. I like to make up my own way of doing things.

Never   Almost Never   Sometimes   Almost Always   Always

17. I would rather tinker with projects than read or write job orders or reports.

Never   Almost Never   Sometimes   Almost Always   Always

18. I need to make lists and develop a plan before I start a new task or job at work.

Never   Almost Never   Sometimes   Almost Always   Always

19. I instinctively want to correct others whose information or answers are not totally accurate.

Never   Almost Never   Sometimes   Almost Always   Always

20. I generate many unique and creative ideas.

Never   Almost Never   Sometimes   Almost Always   Always

21. I feel better if I have time to double-check my work.

Never   Almost Never   Sometimes   Almost Always   Always

22. I like to take things apart to see how they work.

Never   Almost Never   Sometimes   Almost Always   Always

23. I like to discover new ways of doing tasks just to be doing things differently.

Never   Almost Never   Sometimes   Almost Always   Always

24. I seek to read well-documented trade articles on whatever project I am working on.

Never   Almost Never   Sometimes   Almost Always   Always

25. I enjoy reading detailed articles and manuals featuring precisely labeled illustrations.

Never   Almost Never   Sometimes   Almost Always   Always

26. I like the feeling of tools and gadgets in my hand.

Never   Almost Never   Sometimes   Almost Always   Always

27. I keep a neat work area or desk.

Never   Almost Never   Sometimes   Almost Always   Always

28. I am willing to risk offering new ideas even if I know many will not agree with them.

Never   Almost Never   Sometimes   Almost Always   Always

Part II

Answer each of the following questions using the space provided. Write as much as you need until you feel comfortable that you have answered the question.

1. What makes work assignments frustrating for you?

2. If you could choose, what would you do to show how well you do your work task or job?

3. What hobby, sport, or interest do you participate in off the job? How would you teach someone else to do it?

PART III

Scoring Sheet

Name: _____

Return to Questions 1 through 28, and score each of your choices using a 1 for Never, a 2 for Almost Never, a 3 for Sometimes, a 4 for Almost Always, and a 5 for Always.

Next, transfer the score of each response to the Modified LCI Score Sheet (See Figure A.1). Do so by placing the score for each item in the center of the circle whose number matches the item number on the LCI. For example, if your score for Question 1 on the LCI is Almost Always, your score for that item is a 4. Place that score in the center of Circle 1 on the Modified Score Sheet. If your response for Question 2 is Almost Never, your score for that question is a 2. Place a 2 in the center of Circle 2. Continue until you have transferred all of your responses for Questions 1 through 28 on to the scoring sheet.

Finally, add the inserted scores horizontally and record the total in the space to the right of each Scale Score line. These Scale Scores for Sequence, Precision, Technical Reasoning, and Confluence form the Directional Forces of your Compass Rose. Transfer this information to your Compass Rose located at the end of Chapter 2.

Figure A.1 Modified LCI Score Sheet

PATTERNS	2	5	10	13	18	21	27	TOTAL
Sequence	◯	◯	◯	◯	◯	◯	◯	_____
	4	7	9	14	19	24	25	
Precision	◯	◯	◯	◯	◯	◯	◯	_____
	1	6	11	15	17	22	26	
Technical Reasoning	◯	◯	◯	◯	◯	◯	◯	_____
	3	8	12	16	20	23	28	
Confluence	◯	◯	◯	◯	◯	◯	◯	_____

Printed in the United States of America
Learning Connections Resources
PO Box 8861
Turnersville, NJ 08012-8861
USA
(856) 307-7878
www.LCRinfo.com*Insights*/ Res

Appendix B

Figure B.1 Recognizing Learning Patterns at Work

Sequential Pattern

First we will ....
Hold on a second.
We need to get this organized.
Let me finish this first
Then next ....
Where's the agenda?
Wait!
What do you want first?
What are my priorities?
Let's organize this!
One thing at a time.
Show me an example.
Let's use a template.

What's the plan?
Was this on the calendar?
Can we cross that off the list?
Can you take that one step at a time?
Could you give me some directions?
Are there instructions for this?
Where are we going with this?
What do you want?
What are your expectations?
What rules should we follow?
What are the rules?

Precise Pattern

I need more information.
Why are you doing that?
What are you going to do?
What data do we need?
I'd like some more data on that.
We don't have enough information.
Did I tell you about ...?
What are your metrics?
Is that really correct?
What data do you have to support that?
This would be a good six sigma project.

Could you clarify that?
Don't you mean?
Why are you doing that?
Keep me informed.
I better keep that email.
That's not exact enough.
Is this accurate?
Is this reliable?
I'd like to see a report on that.
This needs a white paper.

Technical Pattern

Let's fix that.

How are we doing this?

You don't trust me?

This is @#*&%#@!

Let's get on with it.

Why do you want to know?

Tell me this one-on-one.

Can we please focus?

Just let me do this myself.

How does that work?

Let's just do it!

Don't jump around.

Here's why it will work/not work.

Is this relevant?

What's the bottom line?

What's the principle?

Demonstrate this!

Why is this important?

We don't need a meeting!

Confluent Pattern

I've got an idea!

Let's try this.

Let me draw you a picture.

Just blurt it out!

Let's brainstorm that.

Let's make some connections.

This is like that.

Let's get a picture of this.

Here's my vision.

I just dreamt this up.

This may seem far fetched.

If that doesn't work we can always
   try something else!

There are lots of ways to do this.

What are the alternatives?

Nicknames

Let me suggest this.

Here's another way to look at it.

Give me the big picture.

What's the rush?

Let's play around with this?

Imagine this.

Use your imagination!

How about this?

GLOSSARY

Advanced Learning System refers to LML's system for developing intentional learners. The system includes a specific learning theory (the Brain-Mind Connection), learning tools (the Learning Connections Inventory [LCI], the Learner Profile, the Word Wall, the Metacognitive Drill, and the Strategy Card), an array of skills for Decoding, metacognating, and FITing, and a specific learning lexicon of terms that make up the LML Process.

Affectation refers to our feelings of worth and value as learners. This Mental Process focuses our emotive response to a learning task.

Assess refers to an individual's means of weighing his or her performance against another's expectations for a specific task. This phase in an individual's metacognitive cycle launches reflective practice.

Avoid/Avoid Pattern refers to LCI Scale Scores that range from 7 to 17. An Avoid Pattern has a volume equal to a Use First Pattern. It will make itself heard in a learner's internal metacognitive chatter. When an individual Avoids a Pattern, he or she will feel stress whenever asked to use that Pattern without the benefit of intentional strategies.

Barnacle refers to a metaphor for the types of behaviors (the Excuse Barnacle; the SMTDSLT Barnacle) that can hold individuals back from using their Learning Processes/Directional Learning Processes with intention.

Brain-Mind Connection refers to the brain-mind interface where stimuli, having been processed by the brain, are then filtered by Learning Patterns within the brain-mind interface, and enter the working memory where they are translated into symbols and stored as a part of our consciousness (declarative memory) or subconsciousness (nondeclarative memory).

Brain-Mind Interface refers to the Patterned Processes which operate as a filter of the stimuli passing from the brain to the mind. These Pattern filters welcome, inhibit or limit the movement of stimuli as they seek to enter the working memory to be translated into language, numerals, etc. and directed into any number of memory channels where they are stored for later retrieval and use.

Bridge Learner refers to a learner whose LCI scores fall between 18 to 24 in all four Processes and can apply each Process on a Use As Needed basis. You may hear, "I learn from listening to others and interacting with them. I am comfortable using all of the Processes. Sometimes I feel like a jack-of-all-trades and a master of none, but I also find I can blend in, pitch in, and help make things happen as a contributing member of the group. I weigh things in the balance before I act. I lead from the middle by encouraging others rather than taking charge of a situation."

Chatter/Internal Chatter refers to the internal communication among your Learning Processes as they interact and vie with one another for attention and response as a part of your Team Metacognition. (See Team Metacognition.)

Cognition refers to our internal processing of information. This mental process focuses on thinking, knowing, and understanding and retaining knowledge, data, and facts.

Compass Rose refers to a directional symbol on a map indicating the four ordinal points of North, South, East, and West.

Compass Rose of Learning refers to an individual's ordinal Directional Forces of learning: Sequence, Precision, Technical Reasoning, and Confluence. (See Learning Patterns/Learning Processes/Directional Learning Processes/Directional Forces.)

Conation refers to the pace, skill, autonomy, and manner with which we perform a task. This Mental Process focuses on the *doing* of a learning task.

Confluence refers to the Learning Pattern that describes the way we use our imagination, take initiative and risks, and brainstorm ways of approaching things in a unique manner. Confluence allows the learner to link disparate pieces of information into the big picture.

Connect refers to relating the current learning context to prior learning experiences, gathering and reading information, asking questions, and reviewing previous learning. It may also mean linking up with a peer in the work setting who can model what needs to be done and how to do it.

Decoding refers to analyzing a task to determine which combination of the four Processes is required to complete the task successfully. This is used as a way for learners to Assess how to apply their Processes (i.e., Tether, Intensify, or Forge their use).

Directional Forces (See Learning Patterns.)

Directional Learning Processes (See Learning Patterns.)

Directional Tools refers to those skills and materials that help individuals use their Directional Learning Processes with intention such as the LCI, personal Compass Rose, description of personal Compass Rose, the Word Wall, the Metacognitive Drill, FIT, worksite strategies, and the personal Directional Forces Strategy Card.

Dynamic Learner refers to the LCI Scale Scores of an individual who uses one or two Patterns at the Use First level and any other combination of Avoid or Use As Needed for the remaining Processes. The combination of Use First with the other Use As Needed or Avoid Processes creates a dynamic different from either a Bridge Learner (one whose all four Scale Scores lie between 18 and 24) or a Strong-willed Learner (one who uses three or more Use First Processes resulting in the learner's sense of being his or her own team).

Express refers to the public performance of knowledge and/or a specific skill. This phase in an individual's metacognitive cycle typically follows Rehearsing. Publicly performing the task opens the individual to receiving public feedback.

FIT/FITing refers to matching an individual's Learning Processes/Directional Learning Forces to a specific task by using personal or worksite strategies to Forge, Intensify, and Tether the person's natural use of Sequence, Precision, Technical Reasoning, and Confluence to the specific level of use required by the task.

Forge refers to increasing the use of an individual's Avoid level of a specific Learning Pattern/Process/Directional Force for that person to succeed in completing a specific task. An individual can Forge his or her use of a Process/Directional Force by as much as five points for a limited time. Forging requires intention, strategies, and focused energy.

Intensify refers to increasing the use of an individual's Use As Needed Pattern more forcefully. An individual can Intensify his or her use of a Process/Directional Force by as much as five points for a limited time. Intensifying requires intention, strategies, and focused energy.

Internal Chatter (See Chatter, Metacognition, and Metacognitive Process.)

Interpreting Learning Connections Inventory Scores refers to interpreting the Scale Scores of an individual for each of the four Learning Patterns/Processes/Directional Forces. Because of the interpretation, an individual can anticipate how he or she will respond to a particular task based on his or her Patterns.

Learning refers to our ability to take in the world around us and make sense of it so that we can respond to it in an efficient, effective, and appropriate manner.

Learning Connections Inventory (LCI) refers to the instrument (a two-part, 28- question, self-report tool with three open-response written questions) that is administered to identify an individual's combination of Learning Patterns. Responses to the 28 items are tallied to form four scores representing the degree to which an individual uses each of four Learning Patterns: (1) Sequence, (2) Precision, (3) Technical Reasoning, and (4) Confluence. Each score is placed on a continuum that indicates the range or level of use of each Pattern: Use First, Use As Needed, or Avoid.

Learning Patterns (Directional Forces/Directional Learning Forces/Directional Learning Processes/Learning Processes/Patterns used interchangeably) refer to Sequence, Precision, Technical Reasoning, and Confluence as they make up a person's Compass Rose of Learning.

LCI Scale Scores refers to a visual tool used to present LCI scores of individuals, showing each of their four Patterns, typically expressed in the following order: Sequence, Precision, Technical Reasoning, and Confluence.

Mental Processes refer to the Cognition (thoughts), Conation (action), and Affectation (feelings) occurring in each discrete Learning Process/Directional Force.

Metacognition refers to our internal talk (sometimes referred to as internal chatter)—the voice of our Directional Learning Processes telling, arguing, and negotiating how to proceed, how to achieve, and how to respond by using personal strategies to reach your destination.

Metacognitive Drill refers to the seven terms LML uses to explain what the learner is experiencing as he or she is completing a learning task. These terms include (1) Mull, (2) Connect, (3) Rehearse, (4) Express, (5) Assess, (6) Reflect, and (7) Revisit.

Metacognitive Process refers to the phases of internal talk (internal chatter) that occur among an individual's four Patterns as he or she considers a task.

Mull refers to considering, contemplating, even wallowing in the description or directions of an assignment until the learner is able to understand the expectations of the task and how he or she can make a conscious effort to begin his or her learning. Mulling may take minutes, hours, or even days depending on the nature of the task to be accomplished and the Patterns of the learner seeking to respond to the task.

Patterns (See Directional Forces/Directional Learning Forces/ Learning Patterns/Learning Processes.)

Pattern Combination refers to any combination of an individual's four Learning Patterns/Learning Process/Directional Learning Processes/Directional Learning Forces.

Pattern Conflict refers to the negative interaction of individuals because of pronounced Pattern differences; the conflict is generated because of individuals' lack of communication concerning their differences in how each approaches learning.

Pattern Difference refers to the difference of Pattern combinations between/among individuals.

Pattern Driven refers to an activity that becomes overwhelmingly associated with the use of *one* Pattern not a balance of the four Patterns used in consort.

Pattern FIT refers to the appropriate use of Patterns to undertake a task successfully, the match between the task to be done and the Pattern levels available to do the job.

Pattern Validity refers to matching Pattern Scale Scores to what the person has written as his or her short-answer responses. This process known as "validating the LCI scores" uses a protocol for identifying words reflective of specific Patterns (see Word Wall). This internal validity check helps strengthen reliance that an individual's learning profile (LCI) is accurate for that individual.

Personal Learning Journey refers to the collective set of experiences that comprise an individual's learning history including formal and informal school experiences, work and career experiences, and family and social relationships that have yielded a personal awareness of self.

Personal Learning Profile refers to a record of your Learning Patterns described in your own words. It is a way of translating the Pattern scores into an authentic profile of yourself as a learner.

Precision refers to the Learning Pattern that seeks information and details, asks and answers questions, and researches and documents facts.

Range (See Learning Connections Inventory).

Reflect refers to looking in a handheld mirror, facing oneself, and asking, "Specifically, what did I or did I not do that resulted in this learning outcome?" Reflection is an inward directed activity that reinforces the ownership of the individual's learning strategies and intentional behaviors. This metacognitive phase follows Assessment. This is the heart of becoming an Intentional Learner. This is where the buck stops.

Rehearse refers to privately practicing a response to a learning task. The only audience (and critic) is the learner him or herself.

Revisit refers to revisiting the original learning task, a similar task, or an extension of that task (new assignment) and applying what was learned through the metacognitive phases of Assessment and Reflection. This is where transferrable skills are applied to a specific task with the intention of demonstrating improvement over the previous performance. This is the metacognitive phase that fosters measureable improvement based on the implementation of new learning strategies.

Score/Scale Score (See Learning Connection Inventory).

Sequence refers to the Learning Pattern that needs to organize, plan, and complete work assignments without interruption, using clear instructions as well as a time frame that allows for checking work.

So Much To Do So Little Time (SMTDSLT) refers to a state of living in which individuals allow themselves to be overscheduled and overwhelmed by to-do lists, text messages, e-mails, phone messages, and other demands on their lives.

Strategies refer to specific suggestions that can direct the use of your Learning Patterns to meet specific performance requirements. Strategy selection is based upon resolving the difference between your own Learning Processes and those identified as required by the task.

Strategy Card refers to a charted representation of the gap between a learner's Patterns and a particular task to be completed. A strategy of specific actions is written by the learner for those Patterns that the learner recognizes need to be Tethered, Forged, or Intensified to undertake the task successfully.

Strong-willed Learner refers to a learner whose scores are 25 or more in at least three out of four Patterns. You may hear, "I am my own team. I prefer to work alone so that I can control the plan, the ideas, the talk, the decisions, the process, and the outcomes. I lead from out in front. Sometimes others find it hard to follow my lead."

Team Metacognition (Metacognitive Team) refers to the intentional use of all of Learning Processes to approach any task as a joint effort combining the perspectives, thoughts, actions, and feelings of each Directional Learning Force into a single, focused, unified effort.

Technical Reasoning refers to the Learning Pattern that describes the way we seek relevant real-world experiences and practical answers. This is the Pattern of the fewest words. It emphasizes the ability to problem solve using independent, private thinking and hands-on interaction.

Tether refers to restraining the use of a Use First Learning Pattern. This is done with intention to allow the learner's other Patterns to be heard metacognitively and to operate more effectively.

True North refers to an individual's driving passion or motivation in life—the goal toward which the individual strives, measures life-long fulfillment, and commits significant energy to achieve. It is the defining purpose which drives an individual over the course of a life time.

Use As Needed refers to LCI Scale Scores that range from 18 to 24. The voice of these Patterns is often lost among the more vocal Pattern chatter of Use First and Avoid Patterns.

Use First refers to LCI Scale Scores that range from 25 to 35. A Use First Pattern has a volume equal to an Avoid Pattern. It will make itself heard in a learner's internal metacognitive chatter. Learners use this Pattern first and begin their learning task relying on it.

Word Wall refers to posters or charts that list words associated with each of the four Patterns: (1) Sequence, (2) Precision, (3) Technical Reasoning, and (4) Confluence. The posters provide learners with assistance in doing task analysis and creating Strategy Cards.

Working Memory refers to the memory function that receives stimuli that have passed through the Brain-Mind interface, translates the stimuli into symbolic representation (words, numbers, musical notes, and the like), and stores the product of the translation for ready retrieval within Long Term memory.

Worksite Strategies (See Strategies).

References and Suggested Readings

Alcott, L. M., Meyerson, J., & Shealy, D. (1997). *The journals of Louisa May Alcott.* Athens: University of Georgia.

Bacon, F. (2010). *Essays or counsels—Civil and moral.* Retrieved May 1, 2007, http://bacon.classicauthors.net/EssaysOrCounsels CivilAndMoral/EssaysOrCounselsCivilAndMoral.

Baier, R., & Meyer, A. (1992).Surface analysis of fouling-resistant marine coating. *Biofueling, 6*(2), 165–180.

Baum, J. (2007). Got the baby where's the manual? Respectful parenting from birth through the terrific. Shaftsbury, VT: Mountainside Press.

Bennis, W. (2009).*On becoming a leader* (Fourth ed). New York: Basic Books.

Bruer, J. (1997). *Schools for thought. A Science of learning in the classroom.* Cambridge, MA: MIT Press.

Calleja, C., & Johnston, C. (2000). *Identifying supervisory potential and sources of innovation: A study of human resources within the Brandstatter Corporation.* Unpublished manuscript. Hal Far, Malta.

Campbell, N. (2000). Let Me Learn®: An overview. The Center for Collaborative Research & Education. DuPont Corporation sponsored media presentation produced by *A* Plus Media, Chicago.

Campbell, N. (2003, June). *Presentation in partial fulfillment of accelerated certification in the LML Process.* Center for the Advancement of Learning, Rowan University, Glassboro, NJ.

Campbell, N. (2005, July 10). *"What would you do?"* Best Business Practice presentation, Let Me Learn Summer Institute, Swedesboro, NJ.

Campbell, N. (2007, November 3). *Finding your way.* Annual Conference of the Society of Women Engineers, Los Angeles, CA.

Collins, J. (2001). *Good to great: Why some companies make the leap . . . and others don't.* New York: HarperCollins.

Davies, P. (2007, March 11). *Einstein's god. Speaking of faith.* St.Paul, MN: NPR WHYY.

Dyson, F. (2007, March 11). *Einstein's god. Speaking of faith.* St.Paul, MN: NPR WHYY.

Friedman, T. (2005). *The world is flat: A brief history of the twenty-first century.* New York: Farrar, Straus and Giroux.

Friedman, T. (2006).The world is flat: A brief history of the twenty-first century (Updated and expanded version). New York: Farrar, Straus and Giroux.

Grandin, R.(2007). Personal communication. April 14.

Hallowell. E. M. (2007). *CrazyBusy: Overstretched, overbooked, and about to snap. Strategies for handling your fast paced life.* New York: Ballantine Books.

Johnston, C. (1994, September). *The interactive learning model.* Paper presented at the meeting of the British Education Research Association, Oxford University, Queen Anne's College, Oxford, United Kingdom.

Johnston, C. (1996). *Unlocking the will to learn.* Thousand Oaks, CA: Corwin Press.

Johnston, C. (1997). Using the learning combination inventory. *Educational Leadership, 55*(4), 78–82.

Johnston, C. (1998). *Let me learn*. Thousand Oaks, CA: Corwin Press.

Johnston, C. (2005, September). *Communicating from the inside out*. Keynote presentation at the National Writing Conference, Tumas Dingli School, Hal Warda Street, Attard, Malta.

Johnston, C., & Dainton, G. (2005). *The learning connections inventory manual*. Turnersville, NJ: Learning Connections Resources.

Kounios, J., & Jung-Beeman, M. (2006). Aha! Favors the prepared mind. *Psychological Science*. Retrieved from www.psychologicalscience.org/media/releases/2006/pr060329.cfm.

Kottkamp, R., & Johnston, C. (2000). *A study of plant site operations: Resolving workplace issues using the LML Process*. Unpublished study. Seneca, NY.

MacLean, P. (1978). A mind of three minds: Educating the triune brain. In the *77th yearbook of the national society for the study of education*. Chicago: University of Chicago Press.

Marcellino, P. A. (2002, November*). A team building model for management/leadership classrooms*. Model presented at the University Council for Educational Administration, Pittsburgh, Pennsylvania.

Marcellino, P. A. (2003, November). *Creative problem solving: A teambuilding model for leadership classrooms*. Paper presented at the University Council for Educational Administration, Portland, Oregon.

Marcellino, P. A. (2005a). Bridging disciplines and setting up diverse teams. *Journal of Behavioral and Applied Management*, 6(3), 167–210.

Marcellino, P. A. (2005b). Learning from contrasting teams. *Academic Exchange Quarterly Journal* 9(2), 230–234.

Newell, J., Dahm, K., & Harvey, R. (2004). Developing metacognitive engineering teams. *Chemical Engineering Education, 38*(4).

Nuland, S. (2007). *The biology of the spirit.* Retrieved from http://www.speakingoffaith.publicradio.org/programs/biologyofthespirit/transcript.shtml - 2007-01-18.

Office of Naval Research. (2001, December 19). Battling the barnacle. *Science Daily.* Retrieved May 17, 2010, from http://www.sciencedaily.com /releases/2001/12/011219062137.htm.

Pearle, K. M., & Head, L. M. (2002, June). *Using your brain to build teams at work: A study of the freshman and sophomore engineering clinics at Rowan University.* American Society for Engineering Education Annual Conference & Exposition, Montreal, Canada.

Postman, N. (1990, October). *Informing ourselves to death.* Conference of German Informatics Society (Gesellschaft fuer Informatik), Stuttgart, Germany.

Saxton, M. (1977). *Louisa May Alcott: A modern biography.* Boston: Houghton Mifflin Company.

Schilpp, A. (1979). *Albert Einstein—Autobiographical notes.* Chicago University Press.

Senge, P.M. (1990).*The fifth discipline: The art & practice of the learning organization.* New York: Doubleday.

Senge, P. M. (1999). *The dance of change: The challenges momentum in learning organizations.* New York: Doubleday.

Smiles, S. (1884). *Men of invention and industry.* London: John Murray.

Sobel, D. (1996). *Longitude: The true story of a lone genius who solved the greatest scientific problem of his time.* New York: Penguin.

Snow, R. E., & Jackson, D. N. (1997). *Individual differences in conation: Selected constructs and measures*. (CSE Technical Report 447. Los Angeles, CA: National Center for Research on Evaluation (CRESST).

Sternberg, R. (1996). Myths, countermyths, and truths about intelligence. *Educational Researcher, 25*(2), 11–16.

Sternberg, R. J. (1999). The theory of successful intelligence. *Review of General Psychology, 3*(4), 292–316.

Useem, M. (1998). *The leadership moment: Nine true stories of triumph for all of us*. New York: Three Rivers Press.

Villamizar, L. (2007, October). *International forum for researchers, developers, and practitioners to learn about the best practices/technology in education, government, healthcare, and business*. E-LEARN 2007. World Conference on E-learning in Corporate, Government, Healthcare, & Higher Education, Quebec, Canada.

Zammit, P. (2001, July). *Building supervisory capital through understanding your personnel's learning processes*. Paper presented at the First International Let Me Learn Conference, St. Paul's Bay, Malta.

About the Author

Dr. Christine Johnston has an abiding passion for helping people of all ages understand themselves as learners and using this understanding to improve their learning and their relationships with others. This is her True North!

Although her Personal Learning Journey is included in the body of this text, her Professional Learning Journey is recapped here. Christine's professional life as teacher/trainer/professor has included managing the State of Illinois Department of Local Government Affairs (DLGA) Internship and urban planning program, serving as a public school teacher and administrator, and contributing to research on learning as professor in the Department of Educational Leadership and as Director of the Center for the Advancement of Learning at Rowan University, Glassboro, NJ. Throughout her academic career, she has led a research agenda studying the effects of the Let Me Learn Process® on corporate leadership, learners in the workforce, and learners in formal and informal educational settings.

Her work spans several decades and continents, including universities across the United States, the United Kingdom, Central Europe, the Mediterranean Rim, and Australia. She has authored and coauthored five books on learning, communication, and the Let Me Learn Process® as well as numerous articles and chapters.

Christine earned her BA from the University of Wisconsin-Eau Claire, her MA from University of Wisconsin-Milwaukee, and her Ed.D. from Rutgers University.

INDEX

Advanced Learning System xii, 138, 144, 157

affectation
definition 158, 164
feel(ings) xvii, xix, 28, 35-38, 51, 60, 73, 75, 82, 93, 111, 121, 139, 159, 167

Alcott, L. M. 119, 127, 169, 172

Assess
definition 159
figure 4.2 66
Metacognitive Drill 65-72, 137, 161, 164
self-assessment xx, 69, 81, 99, 166

Avoid
definition 159, 162, 168
figures 3.5, 3.7, 3.9, 3.11 39-42,
Patterns 36-51, 50, 74-75, 82, 90, 94-98

Bacon, F. 1, 169
Baier, R. 112, 169
barnacle
definition 157
description 112
Excuse 117-118
metaphor 111, 113, 116, 121

SMTDSLT 118-120, 122
Baum, J. 80, 169
Bennis, W. 13, 109, 169
brain-mind connection
definition 159-160
explanation 15, 29-31, 60
figure 3.2 30
brain-mind interface 30, 160, 168
Bridge Learner
definition 160, 162
description 51
figure 3.15 48
Bridge Leader
definition 52

Calleja, C. 143, 169
Campbell, N. xi, xiv, 79, 130, 169, 170
chatter
internal 159, 160, 163-164
metacognitive 60-61, 164
cognition
definition 160
thinking 7, 41, 65, 160
Collins, J. 69, 170
communication
among Patterns 60, 160, 165
enhanced 24, 102, 137
failed 18, 130
strategies 86, 132

shrinkage 129, 135
Compass Rose
    boxing xxi, 10, 24, 27, 44,
        49, 53, 54, 76, 103, 121,
        138
    concept 12-26
    definition 161
    examples 55-56
    figure 2.2 25
    internal 15-17, 22, 103
    personal 25, 55-56
conation
    action 6, 23, 28, 35, 60,
        164
    definition 161, 164
Confluence
    definition 42-48
    figures 3.10-3.11 43-44
    in combination 49-50, 65-75
Connect
    definition 161
    figure 4.2 66
    Metacognitive Drill 65-72,
        76, 164
CrazyBusy 119

Dahm, K. 172
Dainton, G. 147, 171
Davies, P. 171
Decoding
    definition 161
    examples of 90, 91, 93
    plant managers 87
    steps to 88
Directional Forces See also
    Learning

Patterns
directional tools
    application xxi, 8, 13-14, 31,
        81
    definition 161
Dunham, G. 19-22
Dynamic Learner
    definition 162
    examples 44-46
Dyson, F. 170

Edleman, M.W. 141
Einstein, A. 14, 16, 29, 137,
        170, 172
Express
    definition 162
    figure 4.2 66
    Metacognitive Drill 65-72,
        85, 164

FIT/FITing See also Forge;
    Intensify; Tether
    definition 162
    tool of 87, 93-94, 99-100,
        102, 104, 111, 114,
        117, 120, 159
flat world
    concept 127-139
    definition 128
Forge See also FIT
    definition 94, 100, 162
Friedman, T. 9. 128

Good to great: Why some companies
    make the leap . . . and others
    don't 69, 170

Got the Baby Where's the Manual?
80, 169
Grandin, R. 113, 170

Hallowell, E. M. 119, 170
Harrison, J. 16, 18, 22, 137
Head, L. M. 172
Harvey, R. 172

Intensify *See also* FIT
definition 87, 94, 96-97,
100, 161,162

Jackson, D. N. 173
Johnston, C. xii, 143, 147, 169,
170, 171, 175
Jung-Beeman, M. 171

Kottkamp, R. xv, 143, 171
Kounios, J. 171

leadership 48, 50-53, 63, 109,
143
*The leadership moment: Nine true
stories of triumph for all of us*
62, 173
learning
definition 28, 29
intention(al) xx, 22, 62, 81,
94 98, 100, 102, 120,
132, 134, 16-138, 159,
166, 167
technology of 128, 134,
136-138
Learning Connections
Inventory (LCI)

instructions for completion
24-25
range 36
scale scores 155-156
validation 45-48
Learning Patterns *See also*
Learning Processes
characteristics 40-44, 157
Directional Forces 15, 22,
35, 37, 40-44
Learning Forces 21
Learning Processes xxi, 8-10,
15-18, 23, 24, 29, 31-
35, 37, 40-44, 49-50,
52, 60, 62-63, 65, 71,
73, 76, 82, 84-86, 88,
90-92, 94, 97, 98, 100,
113, 116, 131, 133,
136-137, 142, 161, 163

MacLean, P. 35, 171
Marcellino, P. A. 171
Mental Processes
definition 164
within patterns 98, 102-103
Metacognition
definition 60, 65, 164
Compass Rose 74
internal talk of Patterns 64,
65, 163
Metacognitive Drill 65-72, 164
Metacognitive Process 164
Meyerson, J. 169
Mull
definition 161
figure 4.2 66

Metacognitive Drill 65-72, 76, 164

Newell, J. 172
Nuland, S. 31, 172

Office of Naval Research 113, 172
On Becoming a Leader 13, 169

Patterns *See* Learning Patterns
Pattern combination 165
Pattern conflict 165
Pearle, K. M. 172
personal learning journey xxi, 3, 8, 10, 81, 117, 143, 145, 165
personal learning profile *See also* Compass Rose; personal
Postman, N. 135,172
Precision
  definition 166, 39-41
  figures 3.6, 3.7 40-41
  in combination 43, 45-46, 49-50, 67, 68, 73-75, 82, 84-85, 88, 90-91, 93, 95-97, 99, 114, 131-133, 137, 144
range *See* Learning Connections Inventory
  figure 3.3 37

Reflect
  definition 70, 166
  figure 4.2 66

Metacognitive Drill 65, 70-72, 137, 164
reflective practice 69, 159
Rehearse
  definition 68-69, 166
  figure 4.2 66
  Metacognitive Drill 65, 72, 76, 85, 136, 164
Revisit
  definition 166
  figure 4.2 66
  Metacognitive Drill 65, 71-72, 75, 137 164

Saxton, M. 119, 172
Schilpp, A. 14, 172
Score/Scale Score *See* Learning Connection Inventory
Senge, P.M. xi, 27, 76, 172
Sequence
  definition 38-39, 49, 50, 166
  figures 3.4, 3.5 39
  in combination 25, 35, 40, 43, 65, 67, 68, 73, 75, 82, 84, 88, 90, 93, 97, 117, 137, 144, 161
Shealy, D. 169
Smiles, S. 18, 172
Snow, R. E. 35, 172
So Much To Do So Little Time (SMTDSLT) *See* barnacle
Sobel, D. 16, 172
Sternberg, R. 173
Strategies/Worksite strategies
  figures 5.9, 5.10 106-107

Strategy Card
    definition 100, 102, 167
    figures 5.7, 5.9 101, 105
    use 119, 159, 162, 168
Strong-willed Learner
    definition 162, 167
    figure 3.14 47
    story 114

team *See also* Team
        Metacognition
    work as xiii, xviii, 22,32, 42,
        44, 51, 102, 130-133,
        137
    Learning Processes as 60, 63,
        72, 74-75, 77, 111
    one-man 114, 115, 121, 132,
        167
Team Metacognition 60, 64,
    160, 167
Technical Reasoning
    definition 25, 35, 41-42, 48,
        167
    figures 3.8, 3.9 42
    in combination 43, 45-49,
        54, 67, 68, 70, 73-75,
        88, 90-91, 93, 95-96,
        114, 131-133
Tether *See* FIT
    definition 87, 94-95, 97-
        100, 161, 168

True North xxiii, 1-3, 8, 10, 11,
    15, 17, 23, 24, 53, 63,
    65, 70, 80, 103, 110,
    114, 117, 118, 134,
    136, 138, 143-145, 168

Use As Needed
    definition 37-38, 168
    Patterns 39, 43, 45-46, 48,-
        49, 50-51, 75, 96-98,
        115, 132-133, 160, 161
Use First
    definition 38, 168
    figures 3.4, 3.6, 3.8, 3.10
        39, 40, 42, 43
    Patterns 36-44, 45-48, 49-
        52, 68, 74-75, 82, 96-
        98, 114, 132
Useem, M. 62, 173

Villamizar, L. 173

Word Wall
    definition 88, 104, 159, 162,
        165, 168
    figure 5.3 89
Working memory 30-31, 73,
    160, 168

Zammit, P. 173

6392602R0

Made in the USA
Charleston, SC
19 October 2010